Inhuman and Heroic Women:
Femininity in the *Odyssey* and the *Arthurian Vulgate*

By: Alexandra Salyga Reynolds
ISBN: 978-1-7751864-2-7
©2016

Certificate of Examination

THE UNIVERSITY OF WESTERN ONTARIO
SCHOOL OF GRADUATE AND POSTDOCTORAL STUDIES

CERTIFICATE OF EXAMINATION

Supervisor

_____
Laurence de Looze

Supervisory Committee

_____

Examining Board

_____
Melitta Adamson

_____
Vlad Tumanov

_____
Randall Pogorzelski

The thesis by

Alexandra Tania Elizabeth **Salyga-Reynolds**

entitled:

"Inhuman and Heroic Women: Femininity in the Odyssey and the Arthurian Vulgate"

is accepted in partial fulfillment of the
requirements for the degree of
Master of Arts

Date ___Sept. 29, 2016___

_____
Călin Mihăilescu
Chair of the Thesis Examination Board

ii

Abstract

The *Odyssey* and the *Arthurian Vulgate* each integrate various traditional sources with various takes on gender into themselves as well as comment directly on the topic. The *Odyssey* prioritizes forming both cooperative and competitive equality between male and female characters and their distinctly masculine and feminine uses of language. The *Arthurian Vulgate* prioritizes forming a status hierarchy with masculinity higher than femininity and correspondences between the gender binary and other binaries, although it also transmits stories with embedded contradictory messages. Both texts also tell a false queen story, which comments on the possibility of a disconnect between a sign and its signified and what each values in a female character enough to make her internally consistent by splitting one complex character into two simple ones.

Keywords: gender, Indo-European philology, False Guinevere, False Helen, comparative method, mythology, Merlin

Table of Contents

Introduction

The *Odyssey* and the *Arthurian Vulgate* have both cast a long shadow over Western culture, their influence reaching modern tropes. The two texts belong to many of the same broad categories: they both have an expansive scope, were composed by multiple anonymous authors, and form intertextual links with a broad range of older and younger texts. They also differ in an essential way: the *Odyssey* is the product of a tradition of oral composition where the *Arthurian Vulgate* is the aggregate of multiple literate composers retelling and adding to older written texts. This project seeks to make connections between these two texts in one aspect: the ideologies of gender contained in each. It will follow each text to its sources, and analyze their use of metaphorically meaningful characters, and notions of textuality to reach conclusions on how each text genders its characters and the process of composition.

1 Sources

The *Odyssey* and the *Arthurian Vulgate* each contain several systems for gendering their characters, one proper to each work and several others embedded within each through its transmission of traditional materials. These sections preserve their source's system of gendering, albeit in a form adjusted to fit the younger text. These internal divisions of the text introduce and allow for differing and contradictory ideologies that relate to gender to coexist. Each text relates itself to its sources in different ways that reflect both the oral or literate nature of their composition and the priorities of their authors.

1.1 The *Odyssey*

The sources of the *Odyssey* are occulted due to their orality, hence their non-survival to the present. These sources are available indirectly through the written texts influenced by them. One of these sources is the Proto-Indo-European story accessible through both the *Odyssey* and its cognate in Sanskrit, the *Nalopākhyāna*. The *Nalopākhyāna* is a section of the Indian epic, the *Mahābhārata*. It follows the *Odyssey*'s main storyline in a linear narrative. Its hero, prince Nala, is chosen as the heroine's husband, their marriage almost dissolving in the husband's absence, and

is reinstated by the same ceremony that enabled his wife, princess

Damayantī, to choose him as her husband the first time. This ceremony, a

svayaṃvara, consists of the suitors participating in an athletic contest set

by the prospective bride, who chooses a husband that did well in the

contest, but not necessarily the winner if they were of unequal status.

This arrangement allows her father to avoid alienating the associates of

his who would become his daughters' suitors by indebting one of them to

himself by giving him a bride; edgewise it gives the daughter some

control over whom she marries (Gresseth 1979). The *Nalopākhyāna*

preserves this story along with its embedded arrangement of mutual self-

interest between the genders in a more primitive form than the *Odyssey*.

The *Odyssey*, as a full-length epic, elaborates on this basic story

and embedded ideology of a mutually beneficial balance between the

male and the female. On the level of narrative, the *Odyssey* is much more

complicated than its cognate. Odysseus, unlike prince Nala, features in

stories other than that of his marriage. The basic story the *Odyssey* shares

with the *Nalopākhyāna* is complicated in order for it to make sense in

continuity with Odysseus' appearances in other stories of the Trojan

Cycle, especially his appearance in the concurrently composed *Iliad*. In

the continuity built by the epic tradition, Odysseus is absent from his

marriage due to his obligation to participate in the Trojan War, meaning

that his initial marriage is now separated from his remarriage by the story

of the *Iliad*. The effect of Odysseus' role in the Trojan War on his role in

the *Odyssey* is felt through the displacement of his first winning of

Penelope.

The *Odyssey* shows the initial winning of Penelope in a

svayaṃvara ceremony through another girl acting out the same story[1].

The girl to take the role of Penelope is Nausicaa. Nausicaa appears in the

Phaeacian episode of the *Odyssey*, which is marked as an otherworldly

place through the closeness of its people to the gods and through gender

inversions in the ceremonial matters in which Odysseus participates.

Odysseus supplicated the queen, rather than king Alcinous as would be

expected, on Athena's instruction. Athena's influence on Odysseus is

decisive to his success at Scheria: she appears to Nausicaa in a dream to

---

[1] This argument follows the logic of Gresseth's 1979 article "The
Odyssey and the Nalopākhyāna" in *Transactions of the American
Philological Association* 109 into a section of the *Odyssey* on which he
did not comment.

nudge her to help Odysseus and appears to Odysseus to tell him how to successfully obtain passage home from the court, both times in disguise as a Phaeacian girl.

The narrative introduces Scheria by way of Athena coming to the daughter of the king of the Phaeacians, Nausicaa, in the form of her friend of the same age to call her to prepare for marriage:

Ναυσικάα, τί νύ σ' ὧδε μεθήμονα γείνατο μήτηρ;

εἵματα μέν τοι κεῖται ἀκηδέα σιγαλόεντα,

σοὶ δὲ γάμος σχεδόν ἐστιν, ἵνα χρὴ καλὰ μὲν αὐτὴν

ἕννυσθαι, τὰ δὲ τοῖσι παρασχεῖν, οἵ κέ σ' ἄγωνται.

ἐκ γάρ τοι τούτων φάτις ἀνθρώπους ἀναβαίνει

ἐσθλή, χαίρουσιν δὲ πατὴρ καὶ πότνια μήτηρ. (6.25-30)

Nausicaa, how comes it that thy mother bore thee so heedless? Thy bright raiment is lying uncared for; yet thy marriage is near at hand, when thou must needs thyself be clad in fair garments, and give other such to those who escort thee. It is from things like these, thou knowest, that good report goeth up among men, and the father and honored mother rejoice. (Murray, 1919)

Athena instructs Nausicaa on how to attract an advantageous marriage through her own actions rather than wait for her mother or father to do the same. Nausicaa demonstrates her merits as a wife by her obedience to Athena in more ways than simply looking better. She demonstrates three skills she would need to use as a married woman of the aristocratic class when she goes to do laundry for herself and her brothers (6.50-101). Nausicaa speaks persuasively in the council chamber to her father, takes care of the household textiles, and oversees a crew of slaves. In these acts, she shows obedience to the goddess, respect to her father, and leadership to her father's female slaves; the merit Nausicaa has is her active maintenance of her social role.

Odysseus enters in Alcinous' hall in time to compete in the set of athletic contests in Nausicaa's svayaṃvara ceremony, which proceeds in a reversed order for Odysseus. Before Odysseus distinguishes himself as a desirable husband in the contests, he is neither chosen by Nausicaa as her husband nor does he ask Alcinous to grant her in marriage as a prize (7.210-328). It is Alcinous who offers that he marry Nausicaa (7.311-316), which he follows up with a promise to send Odysseus safely home. It is after this promise that Odysseus participates in athletic contests instead of engaging in battle with Nausicaa's other suitors after they feel

the need to compete with him since he, like them, is eligible to marry

Nausicaa.

At Ithaca, when Odysseus competes in the contest part of

Penelope's svayaṃvara, he deliberately waits and tests her suitors before

both winning an athletic contest and initiating a battle with them. Not

only is the order of these two parallel incidents inverted, but also the

results. Penelope is married to Odysseus; Nausicaa is left to choose

among her suitors. Since Penelope and Odysseus' story involved two

marriages: an initial one to a virgin Penelope and one after their

separation, it would make sense for both marriages to be included in the

narrative, but the first is not. That suggests that the otherwise out of place

offer of marriage to a virgin princess at Scheria is a displacement of

Odysseus' initial marriage to Penelope.

The *Odyssey* further rearranges the same major themes by

displacing them onto characters other than the main couple, where they

all are in the *Nalopākhyāna*. The *Odyssey* also places the action after the

Trojan War, which complicates the chronology of the poem by making

Odysseus be gone from Ithaca for twenty years but having only the ten

years of the poem's action be accounted for concerning events on Ithaca.

It also displaces the theme of the possible unchastity of a wife from

Penelope onto Clytemnestra, Helen, and the twelve unnamed maids

hanged after the Mnesterophonia; and the first svayaṃvara to the

Phaeacian episode, with the second one remaining in the contest for

Penelope's hand in book 21. The section of the story where the husband

wanders, leaving his wife without knowing if he is dead or alive, is

greatly expanded in the *Odyssey*, where it forms the bulk of the poem,

books 5-13 (Gresseth, 1979).

The *Odyssey* also contains a set of cognate characters split from a

single Proto-Indo-European figure on the Hellenic branch, attested by

their lack of genetic cognates in any other Indo-European culture. Three

characters: Eos, Circe, and Calypso, trace back to the same female solar

figure that abducts and transforms men. Eos is the oldest of the three

characters, deriving her name from the Proto-Indo-European *$h_2ews\acute{o}s$,

literally dawn (Beekes: 2009, p. 492.). The names and epithets attached

to these characters, as well as to female characters in similar roles, each

contain information on the character's nature and the type of aspects or roles she takes in each appearance. Beyond labeling aspects of her character or situation, Eos' epithets, when they appear with her in a day-opening line, also characterize what will happen in that day's narrative.

Beyond her connection to the Eos/Circe/Calypso character type's source, Eos exemplifies the type through her actions; she abducts and immortalizes her lover Cleitus, as told in a genealogical digression in the *Odyssey* (15.250-251). In the *Homeric Hymn to Aphrodite* (5.218-240), Eos tries to immortalize her lover Tithonus by asking Zeus to do it for her. Tithonus receives eternal life but not youth from Zeus, dooming him to age endlessly. Besides the result for her lover, these stories are distinguished by which aspect of Eos they involve. In the former story, Eos the senior goddess uses her power to give her lover a share of immortal society; in the latter, Eos the follower of Zeus asks for her lover's inclusion as an immortal as a favour, presumably lacking the authority to do it herself.

Eos is portrayed these two ways in the two sources to suit their ends. The *Odyssey* offhandedly mentions Eos as a domineering lover who successfully traps her man she chose based on his looks, in contrast with the results of Odysseus' encounters with Eos' cognates, who fail to keep

him. Eos' story is also a foil in the *Homeric Hymn to Aphrodite*, where

Eos' decision to immortalize her lover is contrasted with Aphrodite's

decision not to immortalize her lover, Anchises, whom Zeus forced her to

love (HH 5.45-57). The offhand reference to Eos and Tithonus in the

Odyssey, "Ἠὼς δ᾽ ἐκ λεχέων παρ᾽ ἀγαυοῦ Τιθωνοῖο / ὤρνυθ᾽" (5.1-2),

"Eos rose from bed beside noble Tithonus" implies that Tithonus is

unproblematically with her as an immortal. The *Homeric Hymn to*

Aphrodite chooses a version of Eos and Tithonus that makes both

Aphrodite and Eos equal in their subordination to Zeus, but favours

Aphrodite by showing her learn from Eos' mistake, as befits a hymn in

Aphrodite's praise.

The *Odyssey* also includes an allusion to another affair between

Eos and the mortal man Orion in Calypso's response to Hermes' message

that Zeus needs her to release Odysseus (5.118-128). She argues against

the other gods' bias against goddesses who took mortal lovers with two

examples of mortal man/goddess relationships that ended because of

another god. She attributes Orion's death by Artemis' bow on Ortugie to

Artemis' disapproval of his relationship with Eos, unlike the other versions of his death that attribute it to his arrogance as a hunter (Fontenrose, *Orion*: 1981). Calypso's other example is that of Demeter's lover Iason, who is killed by Zeus' thunderbolt. These stories both blame the death of a goddess' mortal lover on another god with more power than the goddess: one male, one female.

Many of these episodes use the epithet χρυσόθρονος, golden-throned, rather than Eos' standard epithet, ῥοδοδάκτυλος (rosy-fingered), which points towards Eos' status as important to what she does next. The *Homeric Hymn to Aphrodite* and the Eos and Cleitus episode in the *Odyssey*, which have been mentioned above use this epithet. Both describe Eos as acquiring a lover in a context that also fits stories of a male figure taking a lover: a genealogical digression in line with those that trace the ancestry of a hero from a divine stem-father, and a measure of prestige in line with the dispute between Agamemnon and Achilles over Briseus. This association between the epithet χρυσόθρονος applied to Eos and stories where status is being defined is consistent throughout the *Odyssey*.

Circe likely split from Eos slightly before or in the early stages of

the composition of the *Odyssey*. At 10.541-545, Eos may have briefly

replaced Circe for a conventional sendoff from bed scene. After Circe

had finished giving Odysseus directions to the underworld, Eos or Circe

dresses him and herself at dawn. Three lines specifically hold the key to

the passage's ambiguity, "ὣς ἔφατ', αὐτίκα δὲ χρυσόθρονος ἤλυθεν Ἠώς.

/ ἀμφὶ δέ με χλαῖνάν τε χιτῶνά τε εἵματα ἕσσεν: / αὐτὴ δ' ἀργύφεον

φᾶρος μέγα ἕννυτο νύμφη," (10.551-553), "as she spoke, at once golden-

throned Eos came. / She dressed me with garments, a tunic and a cloak

over both sides: / the nymph dressed herself in a splendid silvery

mantle..." These few lines can be interpreted one of two ways: a

formulaic day-opening line preceded by a conversation between Circe

and Odysseus and followed by the same getting ready to leave bed, or

clever editing hiding that Circe is momentarily replaced by her older

cognate, recalling a stage in the *Odyssey*'s composition when which

rapacious goddess would detain Odysseus was not set. The dawn, Eos,

would have risen into the sky clothed in bright white, like the light

emanating from the sun[2]. Either Circe or Eos could be the figure to which

---

[2] Donning a white covering is also a goddess assuming a solar attribute in
this description of Hera: "κρηδέμνῳ δ' ἐφύπερθε καλύψατο δῖα θεάων
καλῷ νηγατέῳ: λευκὸν δ' ἦν ἠέλιος ὥς", "with a beautiful, newly-made

the subject of the second sentence, νύμφη (minor goddess or bride),

refers.

For example, χρυσόθρονος Ἠώς appears as a day-marker when

Circe sends Odysseus to seek the way home from Tiresias in the

underworld (10.487-545). The larger episode emphasizes the difference

between tiers of status: the divine Circe and the mortal Odysseus, and

between the leader Odysseus and his men. This hierarchy is set in two

ways: she is named as a goddess as she directs Odysseus to the

underworld with her divine knowledge (10.487,10.503) and when she is

unseen by the men as she puts the set of animal sacrifices necessary to

contact Tiresias in Odysseus' ship and Odysseus has to explain to them

what has happened (10.573-574). Odysseus grieves at Circe's instruction

that he must go to the underworld, but does as she says anyway (10.496-

502). Odysseus' men respond to the news of their trip to the underworld

the same way Odysseus took the news from Circe; they grieve

themselves but act on what the one with higher status told them over their

own instincts (10.566-568). This instance shows the connection between

---

veil the goddess covered over herself: it was white as the sun" (14.184-
185).

the epithet χρυσόθρονος and status beyond that of its direct referent, Eos.

It points to the concern of the entire episode around Eos χρυσόθρονος'

appearance with establishing a status hierarchy.

In keeping with this flavour of χρυσόθρονος, Odysseus' final

steps towards Penelope on Ithaca are marked by the use of this epithet

rather than ῥοδοδάκτυλος for Eos. Χρυσόθρονος appears when Penelope

instructs her maids how to care for Odysseus in disguise when he has

made it into the palace (19.319). It also appears between Penelope

dreaming that Odysseus is in bed beside her again and Odysseus hearing

her weeping as if she were at the head of his bed (20.91). In addition to

these two steps closer to Odysseus regaining his marriage, the epithet

χρυσόθρονος also marks a step towards Odysseus recovering his

property: he hangs up Melanthius, who had stolen weapons and armour

from Odysseus' store room (22.219). After Athena delays the dawn to

allow Odysseus and Penelope to fully reestablish their marriage (23.241-

246), the final mention of Eos χρυσόθρονος is when the dawn finally

ends this lengthened night and Odysseus leaves to handle the suitors'

families (23.347). Each of these stages of Odysseus recovering his marriage and the property he left in his wife's care that are in the main narrative are marked by day-transitions featuring Eos χρυσόθρονος.

Each reference to Eos in the final six books of the *Odyssey* in a context other than a step towards reestablishing Odysseus and Penelope's marriage or in an embedded narrative uses ῥοδοδάκτυλος instead of χρυσόθρονος. Ῥοδοδάκτυλος appears alone when Telemachus sends Odysseus into town from Eumaeus' hut (17.1) and when Eurycleia tells the story of how Odysseus got the scar by which she recognizes him (19.428). The two epithets appear bookending the description of Athena holding back Eos and night to prolong Odysseus and Penelope's first night back together:

> καί νύ κ᾽ ὀδυρομένοισι φάνη ῥοδοδάκτυλος Ἠώς,
>
> εἰ μὴ ἄρ᾽ ἄλλ᾽ ἐνόησε θεὰ γλαυκῶπις Ἀθήνη.
>
> νύκτα μὲν ἐν περάτῃ δολιχὴν σχέθεν, Ἠῶ δ᾽ αὖτε
>
> ῥύσατ᾽ ἐπ᾽ Ὠκεανῷ χρυσόθρονον, οὐδ᾽ ἔα ἵππους
>
> ζεύγνυσθ᾽ ὠκύποδας, φάος ἀνθρώποισι φέροντας,
>
> Λάμπον καὶ Φαέθονθ᾽, οἵ τ᾽ Ἠῶ πῶλοι ἄγουσι. (23.241-246)
>
> And now would the rosy-fingered Dawn have arisen upon their
>
> weeping, had not the goddess, flashing-eyed Athena, taken other

counsel. The long night she held back at the end of its course, and

likewise stayed the golden-throned Dawn at the streams of

Oceanus, and would not suffer her to yoke her swift-footed horses

that bring light to men, Lampus and Phaethon, who are the colts

that bear the Dawn. (Murray, 1919)

This one passage shows the difference in flavor between the two epithets.

It begins with the standard ῥοδοδάκτυλος, descriptive of the first rays of

light at dawn, since Eos first appears in her usual aspect as a day-opener

after the night had run its usual course. After Athena interrupts this

progress for the sake of Odysseus regaining his status, the epithet

χρυσόθρονος is applied to Eos. The specific context replaces the general

one, and the epithet changes.

Only two goddesses other than Eos are attributed the epithet

χρυσόθρονος in the extant archaic Greek corpus: Hera and Artemis.

Artemis χρυσόθρονος appears in the *Odyssey* during the Calypso's telling

of the story of Eos and Orion (5.123) and in the middle of Phoenix'

speech to Achilles in the *Iliad* to encourage him to return to battle

(9.533). The Eos and Orion episode has Artemis reinforce the status

disparity between mortal men and goddesses, which the affair between

Eos and Orion was capable of dissolving. If Orion had lived, he could have become immortal like Eos' other lovers Cleitus or Tithonus, or he could have become the father of half-human, half-divine children, like Anchises did with Aphrodite.

Phoenix's speech mentions Artemis in a rhetorical parallel to the Siege of Troy: she afflicts the citizens of Calydon with besiegers because their king, Oeneus, failed to offer her first fruits while offering the other gods Hecatombs (9.529-536). This story is made to fit the speech's purpose by Phoenix's attribution of Oeneus' mistake to his "ἀάσατο δὲ μέγα θυμῷ" (9.557), "great intoxication of the heart". The psychic organ he mentions, the θυμός, is the same one he wishes to convince Achilles to control in himself, "Ἀχιλεῦ δάμασον θυμὸν μέγαν" (9.5496), "Achilles overpower your great heart". The parallel between Oeneus and Achilles at this point in the *Iliad* is that they have both, from the point of view in Phoenix's speech, denied an appropriate reciprocal offering to someone in a position of power over them: Oeneus denied Artemis the first-fruits offering she was due, and Achilles denied Agamemnon the military service he was due.

Hera χρυσόθρονος appears in the *Iliad* in two places, when she

seduces Zeus from intervening on behalf of the Trojans (14.153) and

after Hephaestus defuses the tension between Hera and Zeus at a feast of

the gods before they go to bed together (1.611). Both of these episodes

feature Hera in her position as the queen of the gods. The tension

Hephaestus defuses in the episode in book 1 is between Zeus and Hera

over Zeus' support of Thetis, who asked to let the battle shift in favour of

the Trojans in her son Achilles' absence from battle. Hera, as a supporter

of the Danaans disagrees with Zeus' choice to act against them, and as

Zeus' queen dislikes that he has acted on the advice of another goddess

(1.552-560). After this disruption in the status quo of Zeus and Hera's

marriage is resolved without Zeus carrying out his threat of violence

(1.565-568), the epithet χρυσόθρονος is used.

In Hera's seduction of Zeus, Hera uses her status and skill to give

advantages to her favored side, the Greeks. Hera obtains Aphrodite's

girdle from its owner, despite Aphrodite being a supporter of the Trojans,

by both her authority and her use of deception; she asks for some of

Aphrodite's power to help Oceanus and Tethus' marriage and she grants

it due to Hera's status as the wife of Zeus, literally explaining her decision to grant Hera the favour since, "οὐκ ἔστ᾽ οὐδὲ ἔοικε τεὸν ἔπος

ἀρνήσασθαι: / Ζηνὸς γὰρ τοῦ ἀρίστου ἐν ἀγκοίνῃσιν ἰαύεις" (14.212-

213), "it is not seemly to deny this promise: / for you sleep enfolded in

the arms of the best Zeus". Hera goes on to use the element of

Aphrodite's power in the belt to her own ends.

The exact object Aphrodite gives Hera is named parenthetically in

the original Greek, "τῇ νῦν τοῦτον ἱμάντα τεῷ ἐγκάτθεο κόλπῳ /

ποικίλον, ᾧ ἔνι πάντα τετεύχαται: οὐδέ σέ φημι / ἄπρηκτόν γε νέεσθαι, ὅ

τι φρεσὶ σῇσι μενοινᾷς." (14.219-221), "Take now the embroidered

leather strap and put it around your waist, / into which is made all things:

I tell you lest / you go profitlessly, for what you desire eagerly in your

heart". It is surmised from context that the thing Aphrodite gives Hera is

a belt; it is described with the same word used of the suspension of

Odysseus' marriage bed, ἱμάντα, which is a general word for a leather

strap used in any way[3]. It is not a word typically used for a belt for a

woman; that is στρόφιον for a belt worn under the breasts, or ζώνη for a

belt worn at the hips, a word which is a cognate to the word for a

---

[3] It is also used of sandal straps, whip lashes, the draw between the team
of horses and the chariot they pull, reins, and dog leashes.

warrior's belt, ζωστήρ. Both ζώνη and ζωστήρ are derived from *ζώσνη
(Meyer III: 274).

The word ἱμάντα appears only one other time in the *Odyssey*: in
the lock mechanism of the doors to the treasure room in Odysseus'
palace. When Penelope opens it to begin the contest for her hand:

αὐτίκ' ἄρ' ἥ γ' ἱμάντα θοῶς ἀπέλυσε κορώνης,

ἐν δὲ κληῖδ' ἧκε, θυρέων δ' ἀνέκοπτεν ὀχῆας

ἄντα τιτυσκομένη: τὰ δ' ἀνέβραχεν ἠΰτε ταῦρος

βοσκόμενος λειμῶνι: τόσ' ἔβραχε καλὰ θύρετρα

πληγέντα κληῖδι, πετάσθησαν δέ οἱ ὦκα (21.46-50)

straightway she quickly loosed the thong from the handle and

thrust in the key, and with sure aim shot back the bolts. And as a

bull bellows [50] when grazing in a meadow, even so bellowed

the fair doors, smitten by the key; and quickly they flew open

before her. (Murray, 1919)

The strap presumably is attached to a seal on the treasure room door,
which would match the practice of the trade-linked cultures around the
Aegean during the Bronze Age (Younger, 1996). The treasure would
have been sealed with an impression that would in all likelihood have a

sacred significance[4] to protect the goods within. This makes this scene be a place Athena could be in support of Odysseus and Penelope by her sealing of the room from the suitors.

In addition to Aphrodite, another of the gods whose help Hera obtains is that of Hypnos, whom she offers a throne made by Hephaestus, "καλὸν θρόνον ἄφθιτον αἰεὶ / χρύσεον" (14.236-237), "a beautiful, always imperishable golden throne", in exchange for his help sending Zeus to sleep after Hera has had sex with Zeus. Hypnos does not agree to Hera's first offer, citing Zeus' reaction after he had granted the same favour to help Hera act against Heracles when he fought against Troy.

Hypnos credits his survival to another goddess who holds sway over the gods, Nyx, in his refusal. Zeus had chased him to Nyx and:

εἰ μὴ Νὺξ δμήτειρα θεῶν ἐσάωσε καὶ ἀνδρῶν:

τὴν ἱκόμην φεύγων, ὃ δ᾽ ἐπαύσατο χωόμενός περ.

ἅζετο γὰρ μὴ Νυκτὶ θοῇ ἀποθύμια ἔρδοι.

νῦν αὖ τοῦτό μ᾽ ἄνωγας ἀμήχανον ἄλλο τελέσσαι (Il 14.259-262)

---

[4] Religious imagery is common on all types of seal in the Eastern Mediterranean in the time period corresponding to the Late Helladic Bronze Age (Younger, 1996).

had Night not saved me—Night that bends to her sway both gods and men. To her I came in my flight, and besought her, and Zeus refrained him, albeit he was wroth, for he had awe lest he do aught displeasing to swift Night. (Murray, 1919)

Nyx is the recipient of the awe due to a parent or deity from Zeus, as marked by the verb ἅζομαι, which is due to her because of her status as a god of a generation that is older than Zeus'. Hesiod has her be born directly from primal chaos, "ἐκ Χάεος δ᾽ Ἔρεβός τε μέλαινά τε Νὺξ ἐγένοντο" (Hes. Th. 123), "Black Erebos and Nyx were born from Chaos", giving her a great deal of status through her seniority among the gods. This story of Nyx using her status is embedded in a story of Hera using her status; Hera is also referred to as deriving status from seniority in how Hypnus addresses her in his refusal, "Ἥρη πρέσβα θεὰ θύγατερ μεγάλοιο Κρόνοιο" (14.243), "Hera revered goddess daughter of the great Cronos". The adjective πρέσβα is related to a set of words denoting advanced age and high status: πρέσβις (age), πρεσβεύς (ambassador), πρέσβευς/πρέσβεα (old man/woman), πρέσβος (object of reverence). The association between Hera and Nyx' exercise of their influence from their social status derived from seniority reinforces the connection between the golden throne and allotments of status.

Hera goes on to offer another bribe to Hypnos, marriage to one of the younger Graces, a boost to his status that he accepts. Hypnos has Hera swear that she: "ἦ μὲν ἐμοὶ δώσειν Χαρίτων μίαν ὁπλοτεράων / Πασιθέην, ἧς τ᾽ αὐτὸς ἐέλδομαι ἤματα πάντα." (14.275-276), "indeed will give me one of the younger Graces, Pasithea, whom I have desired myself for all days". The name Pasithea is a compound of πάσι-, all, and θέα, goddess. Hera's gift of her can be seen as a gift of everything suitable for a goddess: since the Graces (Χάριτες) tend to represent qualities or activities that are most useful in a situation of reciprocal exchange fueled by the emotion χάρις, which can be translated as favour, pleasure, or gratification as well as grace. Since Pasithea has value beyond the seat in council that the throne represented, she is the more valuable bribe.

A related and less widespread epithet, ἐύθρονος (well-throned), is also exclusively applied to goddesses in the extant literature[5]. In Homer,

---

[5] In addition to appearing in Homer, the epithet ἐύθρονος appears in: Bacchylides (*Dithyrambs* 16.3), Pindar (*Isthmean* 2.5, *Nemean* 3.83, *Olympian* 2.22, *Pythian* 9.60), and Apollonius Rhodius (*Argonautica* 1.1093). It is applied to: Ourania (*Dithyrambs* 16.3, *Pythian* 9.60),

it appears only applied to Eos, once in the *Iliad*, and five times in the

Odyssey. In the *Odyssey*, the epithet ἐύθρονος appears after Nausicaa's

dream (6.48), before Telemachus returns to Ithaca (15.495), after the

suitors harassed Odysseus in disguise as a beggar in front of Penelope

(17.497), after Penelope accepts gifts from the suitors (18.318), and when

Odysseus asks Penelope to have him bathed by an old slave woman

rather than one in her prime (19.343). Each of these contexts is, like those

of χρυσόθρονος, a step towards the reinstatement of the marriage of

Penelope and Odysseus. However, unlike the epithet χρυσόθρονος,

ἐύθρονος tends to mark episodes centered on nights of restless sleep.

The first two appearances of the epithet ἐύθρονος are more

distantly linked to Penelope than the last three. Its first appearance is in

the day-opening line after Nausicaa sees Athena in disguise in her dream,

"ἔνθ' ἀπέβη γλαυκῶπις, ἐπεὶ διεπέφραδε κούρῃ / αὐτίκα δ' Ἠὼς ἦλθεν

ἐύθρονος, ἥ μιν ἔγειρε / Ναυσικάαν ἐύπεπλον· ἄφαρ δ' ἀπεθαύμασ'

ὄνειρον," (6.47-49), "Hither [to Olympus] stepped off the grey-eyed,

after she explained to the girl / at once well-throned Eos came, she

---

Aphrodite (*Isthmean* 2.5), Kleo (*Nemean* 3.83), the daughters of Cadmus
(*Olympian* 2.22), and Rhea (*Argonautica* 1.1093).

awakened her, / well-robed Nausicaa: straightaway she marveled much at the dream". The epithet appears in the context of Athena encouraging Nausicaa to attract valuable suitors with laundered textiles, which are not exclusively clothes: "ζῶστρά τε καὶ πέπλους καὶ ῥήγεα" (6.38), "belts and dresses and coverlets". The attractiveness of all of these items relate to the sexual attractiveness of their owner.

The ζῶστρον, belt, is derived from the verb ζώννυμι, to gird (especially about the loins). The verb is used in arming scenes in the *Iliad*[6] and other texts[7] and in the *Odyssey* of Odysseus meeting the challenge of a resident beggar at Ithaca, Irus, to remove him from the hall by force[8]. However, the noun derived from it is not common; it is a hapax legomenon both in the *Odyssey* and in extant ancient Greek writing. For some reason, Athena tells Nausicaa it is important for her to have "σιγαλόεντα" (6.38), "glossy" girding things. An aspect of the things that Nausicaa actually takes to wash may have influenced this word choice: Nausicaa goes with not only her own laundry, but also that of her three

---

[6] 10.78, 11.16, 14.181, 23.130, 23.685, 23.710.
[7] Aeschylus, *Seven Against Thebes* 1040; Aristophanes, *Lysistrata* 536; Hesiod, *Works and Days* 72; Flavius Josephus, *Antiquitates Judaicae* 1.345 etc...
[8] 18.30, 18.67, 18.77.

unmarried brothers in order to make all of them more attractive for

marriage (6.63-65).

The unisex list of clothing items, and the purpose of the trip to

make both unmarried young men and women attractive for marriage,

meshes with the other purpose of Athena for having Nausicaa do this,

namely to put Nausicaa in a position to clothe and help Odysseus enter

the city and her father's hall without incident. This peaceful entry is in

contrast to the other time Odysseus followed a princess to her parents'

hall in the Laestrygonian episode. Odysseus follows the princess,

daughter of king Antiphates, to her mother the queen, who initiates the

attack of the Laestrygonians, her husband and his giants, on Odysseus

and his men (10.105-120). Neither the queen nor the princess is referred

to directly, either by name or by title, only as the daughter or wife of king

Antiphates and as a maiden, κούρη (10.105), or married woman, γυναῖκα

(10.112); even the spring by which they found the princess drawing water

is named, the Artacia.

This indicates that besides by the lack of Athena's blessing, the

Laestrygonian episode is distinguished from the Phaeacian episode by its female characters' lack of identity. Nausicaa and Arete have strong

identities, each of them usually being referred to by name rather than by

relationship. They perform the same actions as the queen and princess in

the Laestrygonian episode: Nausicaa/ the princess gives Odysseus alone/

Odysseus with his men directions into town and Arete/ the queen inciting

the king to act a certain way towards Odysseus, but the iteration of this

story pattern with identified female characters is both the more

advantageous to Odysseus and the more human.

Nausicaa and Arete respond to and use human speech with each

other, the king, and Odysseus; the princess points out, ἐπέφραδεν

(10.111), with a gesture rather than just words, which would have been

indicated with a form of the verb λέγω, and the queen, "τεῦχε βοὴν"

(10.118), "made a cry" to alert the, "οὐκ ἄνδρεσσιν ἐοικότες, ἀλλὰ

Γίγασιν" (10.120), "not men who lived there, but giants". The absence of

human society among the Laestrygonians is marked by an absence of

women with individual identities and an equal absence of married men/

heroes (ἄνδρες). The two Phaeacian women, however, participate in an

ideal society, which not only affords them individual names, but also affords them a close relationship with the Olympian gods, from which the

Giants are somewhat removed[9], and men with strong identities.

King Alcinous is named as the descendant of a giant, but he does

not follow in the arrogance attributed to the giants who are not kings, like

the followers of Alcinous' great-grandfather Eurymedon. The genealogy

with this information is in Athena's instructions to Odysseus on how he

will approach the king for help; she appears in the form of a girl drawing

water from a spring sacred to Athena and tells him to:

δέσποιναν μὲν πρῶτα κιχήσεαι ἐν μεγάροισιν:

Ἀρήτη δ' ὄνομ' ἐστὶν ἐπώνυμον, ἐκ δὲ τοκήων

τῶν αὐτῶν οἵ περ τέκον Ἀλκίνοον βασιλῆα.

Ναυσίθοον μὲν πρῶτα Ποσειδάων ἐνοσίχθων

γείνατο καὶ Περίβοια, γυναικῶν εἶδος ἀρίστη,

ὁπλοτάτη θυγάτηρ μεγαλήτορος Εὐρυμέδοντος,

ὅς ποθ' ὑπερθύμοισι Γιγάντεσσιν βασίλευεν (7.53-59).

The queen shalt thou approach first in the palace; Arete is the

name by which she is called, and she is sprung from the same line

---

[9] The Giants are related to the Olympian Gods through their mother Gaia
and the blood of Ouranos' severed genitals (Hes. Th. 185).

as is the king Alcinous. Nausithous at the first was born from the

earth-shaker Poseidon and Periboea, the comeliest of women,

youngest daughter of great-hearted Eurymedon, who once was

king over the insolent Giants. (Murray, 1919)

The connection that makes the difference between the Laestrygonians

and the Phaeacians is the one to Poseidon. Athena has put Odysseus in a

position to indirectly obtain the favor of Poseidon, which he lost when he

blinded Poseidon's son Polyphemus, from another of Poseidon's

descendants.

Athena goes on to specify the relationship between Arete and

Alcinous before their marriage, and praise Arete for her ability to

promote harmonious relationships on behalf of women. As for the

relationship:

Ναυσίθοος δ' ἔτεκεν Ῥηξήνορά τ' Ἀλκίνοόν τε.

τὸν μὲν ἄκουρον ἐόντα βάλ' ἀργυρότοξος Ἀπόλλων

νυμφίον ἐν μεγάρῳ, μίαν οἴην παῖδα λιπόντα

Ἀρήτην: τὴν δ' Ἀλκίνοος ποιήσατ' ἄκοιτιν, (7.63-66)

Nausithous begat Rhexenor and Alcinous. Rhexenor, when as yet

he had no son, Apollo of the silver bow smote in his hall, a bridegroom though he was, and he left only one daughter, Arete.

Her Alcinous made his wife (Murray, 1919)

This is a special form of marriage attested to in later Athenian law, an

epikleros marriage. The bride is given away with (epi-) the inheritance

(kleros) to a close relative in order to preserve the inheritance intact. The

virtue of this custom is that it disincentivizes the heiress' relatives from

disinheriting her and gives them a mechanism for coming to a peaceful

agreement over who would marry the heiress (Hoffmann, 1992). The

virtues that Athena attributes to Arete are the value of her inheritance and

the abilities that a person would need to successfully resolve social

conflict through a marriage, as well as handle her position of authority as

queen and a mother well.

When Odysseus and Nausicaa meet at the washbasins, Nausicaa

has already been distinguished from her companions. She leads the dance

of the washers while the clothes dried (6.101), and receives the blessing

of Artemis, who "πασάων δ' ὑπὲρ ἥ γε κάρη ἔχει ἠδὲ μέτωπα, / ῥεῖά τ'

ἀριγνώτη πέλεται, καλαὶ δέ τε πᾶσαι: / ὣς ἥ γ' ἀμφιπόλοισι μετέπρεπε

παρθένος ἀδμής" (6.107-109), "held above all her head and brow, /easily

she was well known, and for all her beauty: / that the unwed girl distinguished herself from the handmaids". Odysseus wakes up just

before Nausicaa returns home with the clothes due to Athena's

intervention. At this point in the narrative, "ἔνθ᾽ αὖτ᾽ ἄλλ᾽ ἐνόησε θεά,

γλαυκῶπις Ἀθήνη, / ὡς Ὀδυσεὺς ἔγροιτο, ἴδοι τ᾽ εὐώπιδα κούρην, / ἥ οἱ

Φαιήκων ἀνδρῶν πόλιν ἡγήσαιτο." (6.112-114), "when the goddess

thought again, bright-eyed Athena, / that Odysseus would awaken, and

see the fair-eyed girl, / who would lead him to the city of Phaeacian

men". The ball Nausicaa and her maids were playing with fell out of

reach, and the noise they made woke up Odysseus.

Odysseus' first thoughts upon awakening tell all of his priorities

for this contact and point towards a parallel with the Laestrygonian

episode:

ὤ μοι ἐγώ, τέων αὖτε βροτῶν ἐς γαῖαν ἱκάνω;

ἦ ῥ᾽ οἵ γ᾽ ὑβρισταί τε καὶ ἄγριοι οὐδὲ δίκαιοι,

ἦε φιλόξεινοι καί σφιν νόος ἐστὶ θεουδής;

ὥς τέ με κουράων ἀμφήλυθε θῆλυς αὐτή·

νυμφάων, αἳ ἔχουσ᾽ ὀρέων αἰπεινὰ κάρηνα

καὶ πηγὰς ποταμῶν καὶ πίσεα ποιήεντα.

ἦ νύ που ἀνθρώπων εἰμὶ σχεδὸν αὐδηέντων;

ἀλλ᾽ ἄγ᾽ ἐγὼν αὐτὸς πειρήσομαι ἠδὲ ἴδωμαι (6.119-126)

Woe is me! to the land of what mortals am I now come? Are they

cruel, and wild, and unjust? or do they love strangers and fear the

gods in their thoughts? There rang in my ears a cry as of maidens,

of nymphs who haunt the towering peaks of the mountains, the

springs that feed the rivers, and the grassy meadows! Can it be

that I am somewhere near men of human speech? Nay, I will

myself make trial and see. (Murray, 1919)

Although he faces the same problem he did every other time he landed

somewhere new, Odysseus now lacks his men, and cannot ask for advice

or send anyone ahead to find out about the inhabitants and absorb the

inherent risk of such an encounter, which is the strategy that saved him

from being trapped by Circe and killed by the Laestrygonians. He cannot

know if he will be led into the city of another savage people, like the

Laestrygonians, or the hall of another nymph, like Circe or Calypso,

without undertaking all of the risk himself.

When Odysseus does come out to speak to the group of maidens,

Nausicaa distinguishes herself again by standing her ground despite the

fact that Odysseus "σμερδαλέος δ᾽ αὐτῇσι φάνη κεκακωμένος ἅλμῃ"

(6.137) "appeared direful to them, maltreated by salt". She remains due to Athena, who "θάρσος ἐνὶ φρεσὶ θῆκε καὶ ἐκ δέος εἵλετο γυίων." (6.141), "set courage into her heart and took fear from her limbs". Odysseus then speaks to Nausicaa, and convinces her to give him clothes and directions to town by speaking to her as the lady of the city and by supplicating her in word rather than in act, since he was too naked to supplicate at her knees appropriately. His introduction of himself and supplication in his first line neatly combines these considerations that are expanded into a persuasive speech, "γουνοῦμαί σε, ἄνασσα: θεός νύ τις, ἦ βροτός ἐσσι;" (6.149), "I supplicate you, lady: are you a god or a mortal?". Nausicaa is moved by his cleverness, and helps him. This encounter at the river, which is introduced through a story with instance of ἐΰθρονος, ends with Odysseus rewarded by assistance made available through divine help and Odysseus' endurance to get to it.

Its next appearance is before Telemachus announces to his crew that he will survey his land the day they reached Ithaca, the action which puts him in contact with his father in Eumaeus' hut and hence allows him to conspire with both him and his mother to rid his house of the suitors, and pay them in town in the morning. The epithet appears in the line:

"καδδραθέτην δ' οὐ πολλὸν ἐπὶ χρόνον, ἀλλὰ μίνυνθα: αἶψα γὰρ Ἡὼς

ἦλθεν ἐΰθρονος." (15.494-495), "they slept for not a long time, but for a

short time: for quickly golden-throned Eos came"; it is followed by

Telemachus' instructions to his men. He tells them to seek hospitality at

the house of the most eager of Penelope's suitors, Eurymachus, instead of

his and Penelope's because of the suitors' intrusion. This would give

Telemachus a benefit in exchange for the hospitality he has afforded

Eurymachus over his courtship of Penelope.

The final three appear in conversations with Penelope, one of her

maids, and Odysseus in disguise involved. It first appears in Penelope's

maid Eurynome's response to Antinous' abuse of Odysseus in disguise:

"εἰ γὰρ ἐπ' ἀρῇσιν τέλος ἡμετέρῃσι γένοιτο: / οὐκ ἄν τις τούτων γε

ἐΰθρονον Ἡῶ ἵκοιτο" (17.496-497), "for if an end comes of our prayers: /

it would not anyway be from them come well-throned Eos". The next

time it appears is in Odysseus' preparation for the Mnesterophonia. He

clears the maids from the hall, telling them that "αὐτὰρ ἐγὼ τούτοισι

φάος πάντεσσι παρέξω. / ἤν περ γάρ κ' ἐθέλωσιν ἐΰθρονον Ἡῶ μίμνειν, /

οὔ τί με νικήσουσι: πολυτλήμων δὲ μάλ' εἰμί." (18.317-319), "myself I

will take light to all these men. / For by it they will wait for well-throned

Eos, / anyway I will prevail: I have endured much". The last time it

appears is during Odysseus' rejection of Penelope's offer of a bath and a

nice bed so he can stay in the hall to better monitor the suitors before the

Mnesterophonia. He tells Penelope that he should sleep in the hall, "κείω

δ' ὡς τὸ πάρος περ ἀΰπνους νύκτας ἴαυον: / πολλὰς γὰρ δὴ νύκτας

ἀεικελίῳ ἐνὶ κοίτῃ / ἄεσα καί τ' ἀνέμεινα ἐΰθρονον Ἠῶ δῖαν" (19.340-

342), "I will sleep as before I lay for restless nights / for indeed many

nights in unseemly beds / I slept and awaited the well-throned goddess

Eos".

   These three appearances of the epithet ἐΰθρονος share a context:

they all mark a lull in active conflict in which Odysseus or Penelope must

endure in order to progress to the active conflict of the Mnesterophonia.

Penelope has resisted remarriage, is persisting in the same at ἐΰθρονος'

appearance, and continues to until she is affected by Athena to set the

contest for her hand (21.1-4). Odysseus endures in the two times his

actions are mentioned in relation to Eos ἐΰθρονος by staying awake in the

hall and observing the suitors in anticipation of routing them at an

opportune time. Even its use in the contexts of Telemachus and his

crew's sleepless night and the interruption of Nausicaa's rest for a message from Athena fit the same broad context as these three, since they both do lose sleep over their role bringing Odysseus home to his marriage.

Its use in the *Iliad* is consistent with this. It appears after the Trojans' sacrifices in the aftermath of their successful day of fighting had been rejected by the gods and before Agamemnon sent the three messengers to persuade Achilles to return to battle. Specifically, the epithet appears when the Trojan horses are described waiting to go out with their owners the next day, "ἵπποι δὲ κρῖ λευκὸν ἐρεπτόμενοι καὶ ὀλύρας / ἑσταότες παρ' ὄχεσφιν ἐΰθρονον Ἠῶ μίμνον" (8.564-565), "the horses fed on white barley and rye / standing by the chariots waiting for well-throned Eos". The part of this context that triggered this epithet is its focus on a safe, at least for the moment, stay in a fortified place before the fighting resumes in the morning. It marks the peak of the Trojans' control of the battlefield, which will be rebuffed by Patroklos and later Achilles himself. Since the Trojans lack divine support, their endurance waiting to complete the rout of the Achaeans is for naught.

In another place in the *Odyssey*, the exact line that introduces the
ambiguous syntax at 10.551-553, "ὣς ἔφατ᾽, αὐτίκα δὲ χρυσόθρονος
ἤλυθεν Ἠώς" (15.56), "as she spoke, at once golden-throned Eos came"
appears in a clearer context. It is the day-opener that forms the hinge
between a conversation about leaving and a scene of getting out of bed,
like when it appeared in book 10. The conversation is between
Telemachus and Peisistratus; Telemachus takes Peisistratus' advice to
wait to be sent off with gifts from their host, Menelaus, before he leaves
to return to Ithaca on Athena's order. The rising from bed scene is
Menelaus getting out of bed with Helen and having her arrange a feast so
he can give Telemachus and Peisistratus gifts publicly. The scenes
surrounding this line at Menelaus' hall at Sparta and Circe's at Aeaea
mirror each other: they are both smooth sendoffs that owe their stability
to a set of clearly defined statuses with their corresponding roles
faithfully carried out.

The two instances of this line are in the middle of parallel
episodes, one focused on Odysseus, the other on Telemachus. Both leave
for Ithaca with the same story. A goddess (Athena or Circe) tells the hero
(Telemachus or Odysseus) that he must leave to return to Ithaca, he

receives some advice that he takes from his helper (Peisistratus or Circe),

then the line at 10.551 and 15.56 appears. The line is followed by the

owner of the hall the hero is in (Menelaus or Circe) wakes up with their

spouse (Helen or Odysseus) and sends off the hero with gifts (generic

prestige goods or sacrifices for contact with Tiresias). Telemachus is set

up to pass the same test as his father in these parallel episodes, furthering

his coming of age by showing him equal his father. This comparison

between these two parallel episodes brings out an aspect in both of the

heroes' hostesses' characters. In contrast to Helen, Circe has accumulated

a monopoly of all the roles around Odysseus. Circe is Odysseus' hostess,

spouse, advisor, and goddess when he is on her island, putting her in an

extreme position of power over him; Helen does not own her husband's

hall and is not a goddess in epic, leaving her in a less advantageous

position.

The frequent mentions of Eos and the use of her various epithets

in the *Odyssey* are associated to a cluster of specific contexts. Her two

rare epithets that appear in the *Odyssey*, χρυσόθρονος and ἐΰθρονος,

mark contexts where the aristocratic rank and status within said rank are

important and are applied exclusively to goddesses. Between the two, χρυσόθρονος is the more common one with a more generic embedded

context, ἐύθρονος is more rare and is linked to the more specific context

of waking up after a restless night from the same concerns as

χρυσόθρονος marks. The two epithets seem to be contemporary and are

associated with similar contexts: the slight differences in their application

may be a function of chance and metric requirements, since they are both

so rare.

These epithets point to a layer of the *Odyssey*'s material from the

Late Bronze Age to Early Iron Age that has two types of adult femininity

represented. One is the powerful female aristocrat who is related by

blood and/or marriage to men of the warrior class, exercises authority

over maintaining the palace of said male relatives, including overseeing

the household's female slaves, wields influence over others of the

aristocratic class with persuasive speech, and can be human, divine, or

partake of both these natures. The other is the vulnerable woman who is

liable to be enslaved if her male relatives are defeated in battle, and

limited to acting through or on behalf of her male relatives with authority

over her.

The influence of the active feminine is marked by the use of the epithets χρυσόθρονος and ἐύθρονος to remind the audience of the influence afforded a mortal woman or goddess speaking from her throne at a feast, and hence is placed in the context of matters of status and the act of apportioning the same that involve a female character. Eos and Artemis are named by one, in the case of Artemis, or both, in the case of Eos, of these epithets: they consistently enjoy a position of power from their position among the gods and exercise their power over mortals appropriately within their sphere of influence. These epithets are applied to Eos in order to mark the action of the day the reference to her begins as associated with these concerns. Episodes centred on Circe, Calypso, and Leukothea are marked in this way, since they use the type of divine power this epithet points towards. Women without explicit divine power in the *Odyssey*, Helen, Nausicaa, Arete, and Penelope are examples of this type of femininity whose action in accordance with the ideal is marked by the epithets. The *Odyssey*'s emphasis of this type of active femininity in comparison to the *Iliad* is one of the main contrasts between their two heroic ideals.

Calypso is a doublet of Circe native to the *Odyssey*'s material, evidenced by her transparent speaking name derived from what she does to Odysseus. Calypso (Καλυψώ) is from the verb καλυπτεὶν, meaning to cover, hide, or bury. While on her island, Odysseus is dead to the world. In Menelaus' hall, Odysseus is mourned as if he were dead, although no one positively states they believe him to definitely be dead (4.212-226). The stages in his journey to Scheria also correspond to a mix of casting off the miasma of death and the stages of a birth (5.228-465). Odysseus sets out into the ocean from the isolation of Ogygia, losing the raft he left the island on in a storm sent by Poseidon, is given a protective sac by Leukothea to keep debris from harming him, and washes ashore up a river. What Odysseus endures separates him from the contamination of death by ridding him of everything that he brought with him from the island, his clothes, provisions, and raft. What happens to him after he loses these things corresponds to the stages of a birth; he begins in the watery womb of the sea, is protected by a veil, which is his amniotic sac, and arrives on land through a yonic river[10] (Holtsmark, 1966). These

---

[10] The river spirit's masculinity (5.445-450) fits with grammatically masculine terms for female genitals like κόλπος in Greek (for bosom and the hollow between waves as well as womb) and Latin cunnus (a derogatory term for both woman and their lower genitals).

stages are repeated after Odysseus covers himself[11] with leaves to sleep beneath a wild and a domestic olive tree (5.474-493), and rises to bathe, and be clothed and fed like a newborn by Nausicaa (6.209-250). The process is finalized when he introduces himself to society by revealing his name in Alcinous' hall (9.19) and tells the court his adventures.

Circe's speaking name is relevant to this point. The name Circe (Κίρκη) is related to the word κίρκος a common noun for raptor or falcon, which itself is related to a word for ring, κρίκος; the connection between the bird and the ring is that raptors will circle in search of prey before swooping down to capture it. Circe got her name from her actions, snatching men like a bird of prey. This avian association of Circe's was later reinterpreted by Claudius Aelianus near the turn of the third century in a passage about which shore-birds will nest near each other in his *De Natura Animalium*, "σειρὴν δὲ πρὸς κίρκην, κίρκη δὲ πρὸς κίρκον οὐ τῷ γένει μόνον, ἀλλὰ καὶ τῇ φύσει διαφέροντε πεφώρασθον" (Ael. NA 4.5). Sirens and circes, here types of bird, nest near each other because "by nature kidnappers seek out kidnappers" (Ael. NA 4.5). By simplifying their nature in order to present them as animals in this passage, Aelianus

---

[11] καλύψατο (5.491).

comments on the nature of both Circe and the Sirens as they appear in the sources available to him, especially the *Odyssey*, which alone features both of them in a narrative. Both Circe and the Sirens act as a rapacious threat to their prey, which is for both of them Odysseus and his men in the *Odyssey*.

1.2 The Arthurian Vulgate

In contrast to the *Odyssey*, the *Arthurian Vulgate* has many sources extant in writing. The *Arthurian Vulgate* arose from a fusion of mythic traditions with Proto-Indo-European roots and High Medieval Christianity. It has several degrees of separation between it and its Proto-Indo-European source, which allows for both the *Arthurian Vulgate*'s direct and its indirect sources to be extant. Its indirect sources, which are the sources of its sources, are Indo-European cognates on the same level of development from Proto-Indo-European as the *Odyssey*. Its direct and one-hop indirect sources' written forms date to the twelfth century and include the *Mabinogion* and the *Welsh Triads* as indirect sources, and the *Lais de Marie de France*, and *Le Chevalier de la Charette* of Chrétien de Troyes, and Geoffery of Monmouth's *Vita Merlini*, *Historia Regum Brittanniae*, and Nennius' *Historia Brittonum* as direct sources.

The *Welsh Triads* and *Mabinogion* contain older interpretations of characters in the Arthurian material than those in either the *Arthurian Vulgate* or its Latin language historical sources that carried this material to an international audience that could not read the Welsh language. The details in the Welsh sources that are not transmitted into Latin sources are not transmitted into the *Arthurian Vulgate* due to the language barrier.

The Latin sources, especially the earliest ones, may also incorporate

cognates to the Welsh versions from other Brittonic languages, Breton or

Cornish. Since the original Cornish and Breton versions of the mythic

elements of the Arthurian material do not survive, only through the

writing of Marie de France (from Breton into French), and Chrétien de

Troyes (a combination of Brittonic sources into French)[12]. The early

Latin historical sources, the *Annales Cambriae* and *De Excidio*

Britanniae, also likely contain Cornish material.

Each of these sources present distinctly feminine sorts of power

and liability that are reinterpreted in the *Arthurian Vulgate*. One of these

that passes down into the *Vulgate* itself is that of a female embodiment of

the sovereignty of a territory. Its older, likely indirect sources, like the

Brittonic mythological cycles and *Beowulf* give this type divine or

monstrous status, depending on its role in the story. Later sources,

including the *Arthurian Vulgate*, humanize this figure. The process of

humanizing the originally divine sovereignty figure corresponds to an

---

[12] Joseph J. Duggan, *The Romances of Chrétien de Troyes*, Yale
University Press, 2001.

increase in the influence of Christianity on the pre-Christian myths and

legends that formed the Arthurian material. To acknowledge a goddess is

to go against the doctrine that there is only one triune God, and although

at first the older polytheistic worldview remained preserved in their

stories, the younger monotheistic worldview was slowly absorbed into

the material. The Virgin Mary's status as a human and not a goddess,

defined in the theology of the Latin Church father Ambrosius, is a source

of the movement towards diminuting the divinity of goddesses in

traditional material derived from Celtic or Scandinavian sources by

analogy. The Virgin Mary is defined as a vessel for divinity, and not

divine in her own right (CSEL LXIV: 122-123); women with legitimate

authority do not own it in the *Arthurian Vulgate*, they lease it from a

higher power.

Grendel's mother in *Beowulf*, an epic in Anglo-Saxon that draws

its material from Scandinavian sources, represents a monstrous aspect of

the sovereignty figure that comes to action as a result of misrule. Grendel

and his mother have been integrated into a form palatable to Christian

theology through a descent from Cain, although they correspond to older

characters that guard the land against illegitimate rule. Grendel's mother is the vengeful aspect of the sovereignty goddess; her son is her forefighter (Sayers 2007). The same set of mother-son keepers of the right to rule a place appears in the *Arthurian Vulgate* (Sommer IV: 90-139), where they are the knight Carados and his mother who hold the Dolorous Tower against Lancelot. In this episode, the figures already turned from their role somewhat in *Beowulf* are moved even further from their origins. It reverses the sides of the fight for legitimate sovereignty: Carados and his mother do not deserve to rule the Dolorous Tower, so the titular hero Lancelot comes to kill Carados and install a legitimate ruler; in *Beowulf*, Grendel and his mother attack the illegitimate ruler, who is helped by the titular hero.

Igraine appears in the extant layers of sources to the *Arthurian Vulgate* from the histories of Geoffery of Monmouth on; she is not in the *Annales Cambriae* or any of the Welsh material. In the *Historia Regum Brittanniae*, Igraine appears as Ignoge, the wife of Brutus and mother by him of the sons: Locrin, Albanact, and Kamber (HRB 2.1), who each correspond to a geographical designation in Britain: Logres, Albania (Scotland), and Cambria respectively. Igraine is the aspect of Britain that with Brutus creates the three regions. In the *Book of Merlin*, Igraine is the embodiment of Uther Pendragon's right to rule Britain. When he takes

the place of her husband, duke Gorlois, to have sex with her, Uther

Pendragon wins against him in battle and becomes her husband properly

(Sommer II: 72-73). After Igraine dies (Sommer II: 78), Uther Pendragon

gets sick and has difficulty holding his land against the Saxons, losing his

rule when he dies of his illness (Sommer II: 78). Igraine is a sovereignty

figure in her brief appearances in the *Book of Merlin* as much as she is in

her source to the book, the *Historia Regum Brittanniae*. Igraine also

follows her husband as a virtuous wife when she comes to him about her

mysterious pregnancy (Sommer II: 73-75); her character blends the

figures of the ideal Christian wife and the prechristian sovereignty

goddess.

Guinevere does not possess explicitly divine qualities in the

Welsh material. She appears in the *Welsh Triads* several times: in the

triad of wives of king Arthur, all are Guinevere with a different father

named (RBH 15), in the triad of harmful blows, Guinevere receives one

that is the causus belli of the battle of Camlann (RBH 12), and was also

pulled from her throne and struck by Mordred at court (RBH 13). Since

she does feature in stories associated with the sovereignty goddess type in works based on the Latin historical sources and the same sources did not

state her divine or non-divine status, Guinevere likely takes these roles

because of the fluid distinction between a consecrated queen and a

goddess that has queenly authority in myth.

In particular, Guinevere's relationship with Arthur's rival,

Mordred is telling. Mordred and Arthur compete for power, as evidenced

by each of them being in the triad of unrestrained ravagings for having

ravaged the other's court (RBH 13). In the *Arthurian Vulgate*, Mordred

attempts to force Guinevere to marry him in order to legitimize his rule

over the land he took from Arthur (Sommer VI: 322-328) Mordred ends

up unsuccessfully besieging Guinevere in a tower (Sommer VI: 349-

353); Guinevere hides from the upcoming battle between Arthur and

Mordred in a convent (Sommer VI: 353-355) and becomes a nun when

she hears of Arthur's death (Sommer VI: 383). The offer of marriage

while Mordred occupied Arthur's land and his subsequent siege of

Guinevere correspond to Mordred's ravaging of Arthur's court, when he

also dethroned and hit Guinevere in the *Welsh Triads*. These references

to Mordred as the other man of Guinevere in the *Welsh Triads* and the

Arthurian Vulgate are both in the context of the competition between

Arthur and Mordred over power. In both the triad of unrestrained ravagings and the *Arthurian Vulgate*, Guinevere is taken as a representation of Arthur's rule: her treatment in the triad matches the treatment of Arthur's court, and the attempt to force her to marry Mordred matches Mordred's conquest of Arthur's kingdom by force.

Marie de France, and her named source of traditional oral Breton lays, assumes a basic familiarity with king Arthur and his court in her works. Of relevance to the stories included in the *Arthurian Vulgate* are her lays *Guigemar* and *Lanval*. *Guigemar* is relevant to the interpreting love stories in the *Arthurian Vulgate*. *Lanval* is relevant to interpreting the supernaturally empowered women in the *Arthurian Vulgate*. *Guigemar* follows the titular knight as he obtains the cure for the wound he got when an arrow of his rebounded on himself as he shot a horned doe, which the doe tells him is the love of a woman who will suffer for him. The doe is described in a manner that marks it as supernatural and both masculine and feminine: "vit une bisse od sun foün. / Tute fu blanche cele beste; / perches de cerf out en la teste." (91-92), "He [Guigemar] saw a doe with a faun. It was all white this beast; she had the horns of a stag on her head". Its supernatural whiteness[13] and

combination of feminine mothering and masculine horns put the doe in a

position to speak authoritatively on the cure for Guigemar's wound,

which is supernatural and involves the conjunction of the genders on

equal terms.

The doe tells Guigemar that his cure will not be any medicine, but

will be the love of a woman:

> ki suferra pur tue amur
>
> si grant peine e si grant dolur,
>
> qu'unkes femme tant ne sufri ;
>
> e tu referas tant pur li, (115-118)
>
> Who will suffer for your love
>
> So great a punishment and so great a pain,
>
> That there is no woman who has suffered as much;
>
> And you will bear the same for her.

---

[13] Whiteness is also a physical attribute of supernatural animals in the stag in the first story of the Pwyll Prince of Dyved section of the *Mabinogion*.
Whiteness is an aspect of feminine supernatural beauty at *Lanval* 107-108.

Since Guigemar does not share this sort of love with any woman he knows, he is left to suffer with his wound at first. After being bedbound for a time, he goes out hunting again despite his pain, and finds a boat on the beach. Guigemar enters the boat and is taken away by it. Guigemar's love who cures him also comes to his kingdom on the same boat (709-978).

This story, whose faithfulness to the traditional Breton material named as its source is unknowable due to the Breton lays' non-extancy, goes out of its way to make the lovers equal despite the difference in gender: each leaves their home for the other, each pines away for the other when they are separated, they both tie a secret knot in their clothes only the other can open, and they are both freed from an affliction by their love, the lady from her oppressively jealous husband and Guigemar from his wound. None of the love stories in the *Arthurian Vulgate* go to these lengths to make the lovers equal to each other; they are too preoccupied with the enactment of the lovers' roles as a lady and a knight in the story.

Lanval follows the titular knight as he is chosen by a fairy lady to be her lover, insults Guinevere by comparison to her and is rescued from condemnation by Arthur by her timely appearance. Lanval is first approached by two damsels when he is riding outside of town, who lead him to their mistress' pavilion; the same two damsels precede their lady into court. The description of the pavilion names it as surpassing those that belonged to Semiramis and emperor Octavian (84-88); the narrative goes on to praise her rich clothes, naming the city of Alexandria as the source of the dye used in her mantle (103-104), and her personal beauty as surpassing "Flur de lis e rose nuvele" (96), "the fleur de lys and fresh rose", but never calling her by name. Instead, the lady who has Lanval brought to be her lover is consistently referred to as "pucele".

The lady of Lanval has the same role as the Lady of the Lake: they are both independent, wealthy, yet unnamed, fairy ladies who are the ideal lady of a hero. The lady of Lanval is this to Lanval and the Lady of the Lake is the same to Lancelot: the lady of Lanval intervenes and saves Lanval when he is in trouble and she can help although he has cut his tie to her; the Lady of the Lake also sends Lancelot help in two critical points after he has left her: after he takes the Dolorous tower (Sommer

III: 90-139) and after he goes mad (Sommer III: 417-420). The contrast

between these stories, namely the lady and the knight's relationship,

shows a difference between what the *Arthurian Vulgate* and Marie de

France consider the ideal relationship between a knight and a lady with

him in her power: Marie de France considers a romantic relationship with

this power dynamic appropriate, the authors of these sections of the

Arthurian Vulgate consider this power dynamic appropriate to a maternal

relationship.

One of the *Arthurian Vulgate*'s sources that underwent this

process is Chrétien de Troyes' *Le Chevalier de la Charette*. In it,

Meleagant, son of a king whose realm neighbours Logres, challenges

King Arthur's court to stop him from kidnapping Guinevere and rescue

the rest of Arthur's subjects whom he has already imprisoned. This

situation makes sense as a metaphor for Meleagant attempting to conquer

Arthur's kingdom by capturing his people and the embodiment of his

legitimate sovereignty. The fact that the Logrians held captive by

Meleagant are kept on the Logrian side of the river frontier between the

kingdoms, as if held under by the successful foothold of an invasion,

supports this idea. Another sign of the challenge's identity as an attempted conquest of Logres is Meleagant's status in his father Bademagu's kingdom, Gorre. Meleagant is subordinated to his father, who is able to oblige him to confront Lancelot on terms to Lancelot's advantage and not to force himself on Guinevere. Meleagant strives to overcome his subordination to king Bademagu, a goal which becoming king of Logres would accomplish.

The whole text of *Le Chevalier de la Charette* is interpolated into the *Arthurian Vulgate*, and later edited to suit its place in the larger work. One such change is the displacement of an incident from the middle of *Le Chevalier de la Charette* to before its section in the *Arthurian Vulgate*. The incident in question is Gawain and Lancelot exchanging a favour for directions to a pass across the river frontier of Gorre, where Guinevere is being held, from a damsel at a crossroads. In the Chrétien version, the exchange is made and the favour is never mentioned again. In the *Arthurian Vulgate*, the damsel calls in Lancelot's favour in time to delay him from immediately rescuing Guinevere; Lancelot properly acknowledges his debt and the rest of this story in the *Arthurian Vulgate* happens as it does in *Le Chevalier de la Charette*. This slight difference between the *Arthurian Vulgate* and its source is telling of the general differences between them. In the earlier version, Lancelot makes his

name by serving his ladylove and queen; in the later version (Sommer

IV: 156-227), Lancelot the knight of an established name and reputation

at court fulfills his obligations to the women to whom he owes service,

which is a lesser prize than that of the earlier version. The story in this

form is repeated in the *Arthurian Vulgate* before the quest for the Holy

Grail is introduced (Sommer VI: 301-305, 317-320), signifying the

transition towards it.

Yvain, the Knight of the Lion, another work of Chrétien de

Troyes, contains an element to which the *Arthurian Vulgate* reacts. This

element is Kay's character: in Chrétien's *Yvain*, Kay is quarrelsome and

habitually doubts and/or devalues the other knights' heroics. The

Arthurian Vulgate rationalizes this aspect of his character with a story

that makes sir Kay and king Arthur brothers through Arthur's foster-

father Antor. Antor's wife nursed Arthur rather than Kay, who was sent

to a wet nurse; Kay's character is affected by her milk, which gave him

his impulsive temperament (Sommer II: 77).

The *Arthurian Vulgate* also drew on Euhemerized legends in historical sources for material. Geoffery of Monmouth's *Vita Merlini*, *Historia Regum Brittanniae*, and *Historia Brittonum* are all historical sources for the *Arthurian Vulgate*'s material. These sources are illuminating for why one character is the way it appears in the *Vulgate*, Merlin, and the changeable set of characters that feature in stories about him. The *Vita Merlini* is one of the sources for the character Merlin, the parts of Merlin and his life included in the *Arthurian Vulgate* is telling of its priorities. The *Vita Merlini* attaches Merlin to the reign of a king not mentioned in the *Vulgate*, Rodarchus, who is also his brother-in-law.

Merlin of the *Vita Merlini* goes mad and retreats into the forest in the aftermath of a military victory that nevertheless resulted in the deaths of some of his men. He is found through the efforts of his sister the queen, Ganieda, who sent her retainers to look for him. One of Ganieda's messengers found Merlin on a mountaintop, drawn to him by his voice as he lamented the coming of winter in verse. The messenger responds to Merlin in verse, accompanying himself on the lyre with a lament on behalf of Merlin's wife Guendolena first, then on behalf of Ganieda, and then segueing into a list of comparisons to heroines from Ovid's

Heroides. The *Arthurian Vulgate* retains the connection between Merlin

accessing the full extent of his powers and living in the forest, but does

not explain it beyond saying that Merlin must live away from society.

Merlin is unable to cope in public but is bound to stay at court by

Rodarchus. In response, Merlin challenges Rodarchus, then Ganieda, to

win his freedom from court in a rhetorical contest. Merlin engages

Rodarchus by inexplicably laughing and exchanging the answer for why

he is laughing for a release from his bonds. The answer he gives is:

> Jccirco risi quoniam Rodarche fuisti
>
> Facto culpandus simul et laudandus eodem
>
> Dum traheres folium modo quod regina capillis
>
> Nescia gestabat- fieres que fidelior illi
>
> Quam fuit illa tibi quando uirgulta subiuit
>
> Quo suus occurrit secum que coiuit adulter
>
> Dum que supina foret sparsis in crinibus hesit
>
> Forte iacens folium quod nescius eripuisti (298-305)
>
> This is the reason I laughed, Rhydderch. You were by a single act
>
> both praiseworthy and blameworthy. When just now you removed
>
> the leaf that the queen had in her hair without knowing it, you

acted more faithfully toward her than she did toward you when she went under the bush where her lover met her and lay with her; and while she was lying there supine with her hair spread out, by chance there caught in it the leaf that you, not knowing all this, removed. (Parry 1925)

Rodarchus gets his answer and releases Merlin, but the value in what Merlin has revealed warrants explanation. The bushes under which Ganieda has sex with her lover is the same one under which Rodarchus did the same, and is likely also the same place, "Velle sub arboribus dum regia sceptra tenere Posset et in populos ius exercere feroces" (239-239), "it would be possible to desire to hold the royal sceptre while under the trees and exercise right among fierce people", that Rodarchus mentions in his offer of various bribes to Merlin as an incentive to stay. That the place under the trees is mentioned as a place for the exercise of authority suggests that the place under the cover of trees/bushes in the sexual context is a place where Ganieda, the queen, is able to affirm the regal authority of her lover.

The challenge of this indictment of Ganieda's loyalty to Rodarchus is met by her with an attempt to prove Merlin's power as a prophet false to Rodarchus. To this effect, she challenges Merlin to

foretell the death of one of the boys in the court; Merlin predicts he will

die from a fall. Ganieda has the boy cut his hair and change his clothes to

appear like he is another boy and then asks Merlin again how he will die;

Merlin says he will die violently in a tree. Ganieda finally has him dress

in women's clothing; "Hec uirgo nec ne dixit morietur in ampne" (353),

"he [Merlin] said this one, girl or not, will die in the Ampney brook".

Rodarchus sees that Merlin has predicted three deaths for the same

person and disbelieves in his power; Rodarchus believes that Merlin is

wrong about Ganieda's infidelity too. The boy goes on to die a triple

death, fulfilling all of Merlin's predictions.

The triple death is a motif that draws on the Indo-European

distinction between the three functions of society that organize social

roles: the priestly, martial, and economical. Each of these functions

corresponds to one of the estates of prerevolutionary France: the First

Estate, the priesthood; the Second Estate, the nobility; the Third Estate,

the commoners. A successful king is praised for how he coordinates these

three sections of society; a failed king or other abuser of regal authority is

punished for his sins against each function, dying for each function. The boy that Ganieda calls, by acting against his king in a role corresponding to each function, sins against them all, and is punished with death for each function. This story is transmitted into the *Arthurian Vulgate*, where Merlin predicts a triple death for a baron of Uther Pendragon and doubter of Merlin's power (Sommer II: 45-47). The version in the *Arthurian Vulgate* does change one thing from its source: where in the *Vita Merlini* the economic function is represented by a girl, in the *Arthurian Vulgate* all of the functions are masculine. This divergence reflects a difference in how the two texts apply gender to the tripartite model of society: the *Arthurian Vulgate* transmits the *Vita Merlini*'s representation of the functions that may be fulfilled by either gender by a male figure faithfully, but does not single out the third estate as feminine like the older text: all social roles are gendered the same.

While Merlin is in the wilderness, King Rodarchus dies in a period of social disorder. During this time, Merlin prophecies from the palace Ganieda built in the Hibernian woods that kept Merlin sane and supplied for him. Merlin prophecies from this palace and after the prophetic utterances recorded in the *Vita Merlini*, Ganieda acquires his ability; Merlin is relieved of his duty of relaying predictions to society by her. The character in the *Arthurian Vulgate* who corresponds to Ganieda as the student of Merlin who keeps him in the place she built to retire permanently from life at court is Viviane. Viviane is the ladylove of Merlin, who takes advantage of her relationship with him to learn enchantments. Merlin is rendered helpless by his feelings for her, and teaches her the skills that would allow her sexually dominate him despite knowing the eventual results: Viviane avoids having sex with him by magic before she can entrap him in an invisible tower to visit as she pleases (Sommer II: 280, 376, 421, 451-452).

These two ends to Merlin's career follow the same trajectory for him: Merlin is enclosed in a structure built by the most important woman in his life who has also gained the same magical powers as him. The version in the *Vita Merlini* has the conflict between Merlin and Ganieda be resolved: now that Ganieda is no longer queen, the threat of Merlin's insight to her position is neutralized, leaving Ganieda free to look after her self-interest by retiring from public life. She had lost the protection against the force of other men that her husband afforded her from his role in the warrior function, so she acquired the divine protection of the priestly function by becoming a prophetess. Both Merlin and Ganieda follow the same path, leaving their role in class devoted to the martial

function to a new one as a prophet of the sacral function.

The version in the *Arthurian Vulgate* has Merlin's enclosure at

the end of his relationship with Arthur and his court be an act of

domination on his ladylove's part (Sommer II: 451-452). Merlin has the

same fate as in the *Vita Merlini*, but with the final balance and

reconciliation between the two genders of older version replaced with

one winning over the other. Instead of the exchanges between Ganieda

and Merlin and negotiations of power between them, Viviane captures

Merlin for her pleasure and Merlin accepts this end to his career as

preordained due to his supernatural insight without any negotiation or

exchange between them. Viviane's motivations for her actions are only

explained in the narrative as the inevitable end to Merlin's influence at

court.

In the *Vita Merlini*, Merlin acts out the same story as Odysseus

and Penelope do in the *Odyssey* with his wife Guendolena. He leaves his

wife for the forest with permission to remarry in his absence; if he finds

her with her new husband at a formal wedding feast, he promises to attend it peaceably, however, if he finds her lover before they are

formally married, he promises to kill him (375-386). Merlin visits

Guendolena's palace in time to see the bridegroom on the night before

the wedding ceremony, and kills him on sight to retain her as his wife

(422-463). Relevant to the parallel with the *Odyssey* is a parallel to the

Nalopākhyāna; in the *Nalopākhyāna*, prince Nala is separated from his

wife by an exile to the forest. The two cultures that developed from

Proto-Indo-European in areas where the forest was the place of isolation

and travel rather than the sea, the Indo-European Indians and the Celts,

used the forest as the place where the abandoning spouse goes; the

Hellenes, with mountains and the sea as wild places, and mountains being

inhospitable to travel, separated their hero from his wife with the sea.

All three of these stories focus on the ambiguous status of a wife

with an absent husband. On the Indic side, there are several extant

legalistic sources detailing the confusion about what the acceptable

actions of a wife in the absence of her husband were. They disagree over

how long she should await her husband's return before the marriage can

be considered dissolved, if she should seek news of her husband and what

effect news would have on her position, if she should seek to remarry after waiting, if the marriage arrangement should be from her relatives or she should seek a new husband herself, and how she should support herself financially during the wait (Jamison 1999). The *Odyssey* shows several solutions to the ambiguity: Clytemnestra arranges her own remarriage in Agamemnon's absence, Penelope delays her suitors by starting the waiting period at the last news of Odysseus and seeking news of him (Jamison 1999).

The presence of a story based on this ambiguity in the status of a wife absent her husband in these three places suggests that they have their roots in at least one Indo-European story that exploits the same for conflict; there are too many confounding factors to state with certainty if there is one source or several closely connected sources that take various stances within this categorical ambiguity in Proto-Indo-European. This comparison also suggests that Merlin may have been a king before he became a prophet in some versions of his story; Merlin's kingship also gives another reason for the triple death of the boy Ganieda set up to prove Merlin false, he is acting both to deceive king Rodarchus and directly against Merlin, whose kingship is likely in the sources rather than explicitly in the text of the *Vita Merlini*, since Merlin is never

directly called a king in the *Vita*.

Neither Ganieda nor Guendolena is a character in the *Arthurian*

Vulgate; Merlin instead interacts with his unnamed mother and his

ladylove Viviane. The shift in Merlin's relationships with the two main

women in his life reveals a difference in the two texts' attitudes towards

the gendering of persuasive intelligence. In the *Vita Merlini*, both Merlin

and his sister are capable of the same feats of superhuman intelligence.

The book only records Merlin's prophecies, but it leaves Ganieda with

the power. Merlin as well as Ganieda enjoys a position of power sexually

over their spouse: Merlin is able to hold his wife bound in marriage to

him despite his retirement to the forest, and Ganieda is able to cheat on

her husband without consequence. This model of different but equal

power between the genders, presented by the final state of Merlin and

Ganieda, is replaced in the *Arthurian Vulgate* by one of domination of

one by the other, represented by Merlin's final state in Viviane's power.

Viviane corresponds to Ganieda, since they both compete with Merlin

before they are with him in the state he is in his final appearance in the

text. Ganieda and Merlin compete during the triple death prediction;

Viviane and Merlin compete for power in the relationship without an external object, revealing this versions derivation from an older text that included a motivation for their competition and a concern with organizing the genders into a status hierarchy.

The *Historia Brittonum* has a character Ambrosius, the son of a spirit and a highborn damsel who had defensively entered a convent, explain to Vortigern that even if he sacrifices him to keep Vortigern's tower up, the tower will still fall due to the combat of two serpents underground (40-42). The same story is attributed to Merlin in the *Historia Regum Brittanniae*, with the name Ambrosius explained as an alternate name for Merlin (6.18-19). The *Historia Regum Brittanniae* seems to have latched onto the originally separate character of Ambrosius and fused it to Merlin, giving Merlin his origin from the union of a woman and a demon and a natural explaination for his powers.

The *Historia Regum Brittanniae* includes both Merlin and Guendolena, but gives Guendolena a completely different biography than the *Vita Merlini* (2.2-6) and gives an account of Merlin's birth (6.18-19), which the *Vita* lacks. In the *Historia Regum Brittanniae*, Guendolena is the daughter of Corineus, who at Corineus' insistence married Locrin

instead of the highborn captive that Locrin won from the king of the

Huns and fell in love with, Estrildis. Locrin keeps Estrildis as a lover in

secret while Corineus is alive, but after he dies Locrin divorces

Guendolena and attempts to make Estrildis queen; he is thwarted by

Guendolena, who raises an army in Cornwall and fights him. Locrin dies

in battle, and Guendolena has Estrildis and her daughter by Locrin,

Sabre, drowned in the Severn, which the narrative explains as taking its

name from Sabre's. Guendolena rules Logres and Cornwall until she

retires to Cornwall upon her son, Madden's, maturity. This Guendolena is

placed in a different generation than Merlin, but she can be identified

with the Guendolena who appears in the *Vita Merlini* because the two are

both queens with the same name who feature in a story about a dispute

over marriage and sovereignty. Merlin's marriage to Guendolena is an

expression of his kingship before he abandons it in his madness and

becomes a prophet.

The *Arthurian Vulgate* has Merlin explicitly derive his powers of

supernatural knowledge and persuasive rhetoric from his demon father

unlike the historical sources, which name Merlin a prophet whose insights are presumably divinely inspired. The *Vita Merlini* has a Merlin whose powers are divine: he is referred to by the word vates, prophet, which is used in Classical Latin to refer to prophets of the various gods known throughout the Roman Empire and the associated verb, vaticinare, is the standard term in the Vulgate version of the Bible to describe the prophets making predictions inspired by the God of Christianity. His birth from a holy woman and a partially angelic and partially human spirit *Historia Regum Brittanniae* explicitly explains Merlin's supernatural insight as divinely sourced. However, when the story of Merlin's birth is told in the *Arthurian Vulgate*, his father is not a spirit on the side of God who is willingly accepted as a lover by Merlin's mother like in the *Historia Regum Brittanniae* (6.18), but a demon who gains access to her house due to female sin in it and forces himself on her in order to beget the antichrist (Sommer II: 3-10).

Merlin's birth in the *Arthurian Vulgate* is described as the result of a violation of the sexual mores and duties to her family expected of a woman in the *Book of Lancelot* (Sommer III: 20-21), and in the *Book of Merlin* (Sommer II: 3-14), as the result of the demonic interference, with virtueless femininity not to blame. The ideal for a woman of reproductive age that this story in these two forms engages with is the one set out in the Book of Timothy:

> Adolescentiores autem viduas devita: cum enim luxuriatæ fuerint in Christo, nubere volunt: habentes damnationem, quia primam fidem irritam fecerunt; simul autem et otiosæ discunt circuire domos: non solum otiosæ, sed et verbosæ, et curiosæ, loquentes quæ non oportet. Volo ergo juniores nubere, filios procreare, matresfamilias esse, nullam occasionem dare adversario maledicti gratia. Jam enim quædam conversæ sunt retro Satanam. (1 Timothy 5.11-15)

> But the younger widows refuse: for when they have begun to wax wanton against Christ, they will marry; Having damnation, because they have cast off their first faith. And withal they learn to be idle, wandering about from house to house; and not only idle, but tattlers also and busybodies, speaking things which they ought not. I will therefore that the younger women marry, bear children, guide the house, give none occasion to the adversary to speak reproachfully. For some are already turned aside after Satan.

The version in the *Book of Lancelot* has Merlin's mother willingly turn towards Satan; the version of the *Book of Merlin* has the demons incessantly pressure Merlin's mother in order to make her give in. They kill her father's livestock as well as her father and her brother, make her mother kill herself, cause her one sister to be buried alive for having sex to a unique lover outside of marriage, and her other sister to become promiscuous before they can make her vulnerable enough to beget Merlin. After she gives birth and Merlin's supernatural nature is obvious, his mother is the target of gossip (Sommer II: 15-16). Instead of engaging in virtueless femininity, Merlin's mother is tormented by it in the *Book of Merlin*.

A woman's faith to her husband reflects her faith to God in this ideal: if she falls short in her role towards her husband and children, she turns to Satan. A man is subject to scrutiny of his marriage and relationship with his children only when he is considered for the holy office of Bishop (1 Timothy 3.2-4) or Deacon (1 Timothy 3.8-12); a man in each of these positions must, in addition to showing virtue himself, have a virtuous wife, obedient children, be the master of his household, and have only been the husband of one wife. Timothy also names the act of "prohibentium nubere" (1 Timothy 4.3), "forbidding to marry" as an action that will be taken from heeding "doctrinis dæmoniorum" (1

Timothy 4.1), "the doctrines of devils". This interdiction against

forbidding marriage is followed in the sections of the *Arthurian Vulgate*

set in the early period of the Church, and is not reconciled with the

contemporary practices of religious asceticism that forbid marriage and

are incorporated into the sections of the *Vulgate* that take place during

and near king Arthur's reign.

The contrast between these two attitudes towards the potential for

virtue in marriage is almost lost among other differences by an aggregate

of narrative choices of the *Arthurian Vulgate*'s authors. The two

attitudes: the older one that considered an ideologically correct marriage

a state conducive to spiritual progress and the younger one that

considered marriage and any other contact with the world antithetical to

the same. In the *Arthurian Vulgate*, the men: Joseph of Arimathea,

Evalach/Mordrain, and Seraphe/Nacien and their wives: Joseph's

unnamed wife, Sarrasinte, and Flegentine, reconcile their piety with their

single marriage to one spouse over their lifetime.

Each of the wives chooses to have no husband other than the one

they have, forsaking the opportunity to remarry or protect their material security in another way in his absence due to the demands of his duty to God. Joseph of Arimathea's wife chooses not to remarry for thirty years (Sommer I: 17) while Joseph is kept miraculously safe in the pillar in which he was sealed to die (Sommer I: 15). Despite her estimation of Evalach's character: "il est vns moult crueus hom" (Sommer I: 72), "he is a very cruel man", Sarrasinte still seeks divine help for him from Josephus after revealing she has been a Christian since childhood (Sommer I: 66-73). Flegentine seeks her husband instead of seeking to protect her land and status as a landowner when Nacien is imprisoned by the same non-Christian who threatens her land (Sommer I: 111-113). Sarrasinte also remains faithful to her husband despite his mysterious disappearance (Sommer I: 87, 111).

Flegentine goes further than Sarrasinte and actually leaves to attempt to find her husband Nacien when he vanishes by act of God (Sommer I: 113). She departs on the same mission as the many knights sent questing after another, but since she is a lady she must conceal her intent to look for Nacien as intent to go visit Sarrasinte as she leaves. Flegentine does not accomplish anything by seeking him either; she hears of his return and goes to him. This half-story, a setup without a payoff, is telling of the authors' attitudes: on one hand, a man and a woman's devotion to an appropriate object is equally valuable, on the other, independant questing is the role of the knight errant. The narrative splits the difference between having the lady Flegentine equal the devotion of a vassal knight to his lord with her devotion to her lord and husband and leaving her in the conventional state of passive waiting like Sarrasinte.

The men demonstrate their loyalty to God: Joseph by giving Jesus an honorable burial, Evalach accepts conversion for himself and Sarras and endures testing on the rock as Mordrain, and Nacien endures capture and torment by Calafer as a result of his conversion and does not give up Christianity. The wives demonstrate their loyalty to their husbands as well as to God, both becoming Christians and each adhering to their one husband; in contrast to the men, the women's actions are directed towards their husbands rather than God, rejecting the opportunity to forward their self-interest by living independently or remarrying upon their husband's disappearance.

Another character in the *Arthurian Vulgate* who is radically reinterpreted from their sources is Morgan. Morgan first appears by name in the *Vita Merlini*, where she is named as Morgen (920, 933) and praised

extensively in one of Merlin's prophecies as a skilled surgeon (915-940).

She also appears in the *Yvain, or the Knight of the Lion* of Chrétien de

Troyes as the "Margue la sage" (86c.2921), "Margue the Wise" who gave

the Lady of Noroison the ointment her maid used to heal Yvain's

madness. Neither of these mentions Morgen/Margue's parentage, other

relations, social position, or place of birth or land ownership. Because of

her mention by name in these texts, her access to the education needed to

excel as a healer, and her relationship with the Lady of Noroison in

Chrétien, she is of the aristocratic class. The fact that Morgan is

mentioned in both texts in relation to her abilities says that they are her

greatest source of status, which can be interpreted to mean that she is

unmarried, or has a husband who is of lesser status than her, and/or that

she is the most well-known of her immediate relatives other than her

husband to make this framing of her character appropriate.

Morgan was likely poorly connected to the Arthurian material in

its disparate forms throughout its sources; her introduction to the material

via a prophecy of Merlin's is the best evidence for this. If she were

already well connected to Merlin or to any of the kings of Britain she would appear in the historical sources as such and it would have been mentioned in her praise in the *Vita Merlini*. In the *Arthurian Vulgate*, Morgan is given much of what she lacked in biographical details in the older texts, although they disagree over whether she is the full sister or half sister of Arthur, or half sister through Igraine or through Uther Pendragon, or if she is the mother of Mordred.

Morgan's skills as a physician do not follow her into the *Arthurian Vulgate*, instead she has powers of enchantment learned from Merlin (Sommer II: 254). She also uses natural means to rival Guinevere: Morgan first quarrels with her over Guinevere's interference in her affair with Guinevere's cousin Guiomar (Sommer IV: 117-124), and she finally wins against Guinevere when she convinces Arthur of the truth of Guinevere's adultery with Lancelot (Sommer VI: 237-242). Morgan is generally more quarrelsome and not as well respected in the *Arthurian Vulgate* as she is in the earlier sources. This may reflect the position of a physician being gendered as masculine by the authors, and thus inappropriate for a woman; sorcery is a power that is feminine be unproblimatically given to a woman, and the tension that the change created generated the distaste with which she was characterized.

The Lady of the Lake[14] aggregates the roles and abilities that,

while forming a part of the traditional material, were inconvenient to the

newer texts' conceptions of gender. The Lady of the Lake possesses both

magical and temporal power, and she substitutes for female characters

when they enter a position of temporal powerlessness and spiritual

power. Women, unlike men, do not stay in a state of both religious and

secular power. They possess one or the other at one time: as a queen with

secular authority, a nun with Christian religious authority, or as a fey

with religious authority from prechristian sources.

In particular, the Lady of the Lake substitutes for the queens

Evaine and Elaine, the mothers of Lancelot, Bors, and Ban, acting as a

surrogate mother for the boys in the aftermath of king Claudas' conquest

of kings Bors and Ban's kingdoms. Evaine and Elaine are not dead like

their husbands; they have simply entered a convent in order to prevent

Claudas from harming them (Sommer III: 15-19). Their survival in a

---

[14] The Lady of the Lake is named at her introduction in *Lancelot I* as the same Viviane Merlin taught magic (Sommer III: 21), which is her only name in the *Arthurian Vulgate*. Later sources name her differently; even the closest one temporally, the *Post-Vulgate Cycle*, which calls her Ninianne.

convent, like that of Guinevere, is a way to have them leave the world

without their death, and suggests that an actual death was an

inappropriate way to end their stories. Evaine (Sommer III: 207)

eventually does die, but a reason for this hesitancy for Guinevere and

Elaine may be that there was association between their characters and

immortality that made the authors of the *Arthurian Vulgate* consider a

narrative of their deaths too far outside of tradition to add.

The Lady of the Lake first takes the only son of the elder king,

Lancelot, (Sommer III: 14) and later rescues his cousins from king

Claudas by sending her damsel (Sommer III: 48-57). This woman is

named twice in the *Arthurian Vulgate*, the first time (Sommer III: 48) her

name is Saraide, the second time (Sommer III: 374) her name is Celise.

The two passages definitely refer to the same character. The two names

are the product of two different authorial hands, each of which was likely

unaware of the other. This unawareness is made more likely by the rarity

of the Damsel of the Lake's name: she is only referred to by name in

these two places; it would be easy to have lost track of the older name in

Lancelot I in its sheer, unstructured volume when it came time to mention

her by name again, but it is likely that she was named by two different authorial hands. The name Saraide is marked as the correct name, which

is likely an addition after the name Celise had been attributed to her.

The disagreement over Damsel of the Lake's name, combined

with her habitual identity by position and lack of presence outside of the

Arthurian Vulgate, says that she is a character native to the text. If she

were an established character before her appearance in the *Arthurian*

Vulgate, she would have a consistent name, since the *Arthurian Vulgate*'s

sources more consistently name their female characters. The Damsel of

the Lake's character is probably an import of the Scandinavian shield

maiden[15]. She leads the rescue of Bors and Ban from king Claudas by

both engaging in a violent confrontation against Claudas and by using her

lady's trick of switching the appearance of the boys with that of two

greyhounds (Sommer III: 48-57).

Another source of material for the *Arthurian Vulgate* is the Bible.

One section that retells a Biblical story is the testing of king Mordrain on

---

[15] The authors had access to examples in Latin in the *Gesta Danorum* of
Saxo Grammaticus, which mentions two female aristocratic warriors of
the Danes, Hetha and Wisna, introduced in book 8 (Holder: 258), and
given sporadic mentions after this point.

the rock (Sommer I: 88-107), which retells the temptation of Christ in the

desert. Like Jesus does in the extended versions of this story in Matthew

and Luke (Matt 4, Luke 4), Mordrain converses with the Devil and stays

true to God by rejecting the Devil's bribes, disbelieving his lies, fasting,

and praying. In the Bible, Jesus rejects the Devil's offers of jewels and

worldly power, and ignores his idle threats. Mordrain resists the same

temptations and threats on the rock (Sommer I: 100-101).

The *Arthurian Vulgate* also contains characters and places

expanded out of details of the simple form of the story and backwritten a

false etymology with ancient origins. One place with such a false

etymology is the city of Sarras, which king Evalach rules and converts to

Christianity after his own conversion by Josephus. Sarras is named as the

source of the name Saracen for the followers of Mohammed instead of

Sarah, wife of Abraham in the *Vulgate* (Sommer I: 21). Sarrasinte, the

queen of king Evalach, has a name that is clearly derived from Sarras

with the addition of a feminine suffix –inte by analogy with Latin-derived

nouns in the contemporary Middle French that were derived from

gerunds marked by the masculine or feminine –ntis suffix, but the

connection is not explained in the narrative. The name Sarras is likely derived from Saracen rather than the other way around as it is in the text. There is a real place in Southern France on the Rhône called Sarras, which could have acquired its name from the Umayyad invasion of Gaul in the eighth century (Joëlle Dupraz et Christel Fraisse: 1985). It is first mentioned by name in a grant of land to the Abbey of St-André de Vienne in 1037 as a "Villa sarratoria" (Albin Mazon: 1901), meaning it existed in time to influence the twelfth-century authors of the *Arthurian Vulgate*. In the *Arthurian Vulgate*, however, Sarras is in the Levant, within a few days' walking distance for Josephus and his followers from Jerusalem (Sommer I: 19-21).

The queen's actual origin as an embodiment of Sarras is disavowed in the same context as a denial of the matriarch Sarah's authority to name a people; the text goes out of its way to separate the queen from her two sources of authority that are reinforced as legitimate in other stories in the *Arthurian Vulgate*: her embodiment of the king's right to rule a specific place and her authority over her children. This separation of Sarrasinte from her power is also present in the story of her conversion to Christianity with and at the behest of her mother (Sommer I: 67-69). Sarrasinte is defined as a virtuous Christian queen by her surrender of her agency: she converts as the result of a promise to do whatever the hermit who healed her mother said in exchange for his help and she is not given the authority of an embodiment of legitimate rule over Sarras over her husband's continued temporal power. The only hint that Sarrasinte has any power to negotiate her relationship with her husband is her promise to convince him to convert if Josephus helped him return safely from battle (Sommer I: 67); this promise comes to nothing, since king Evalach converts after he is saved by angel in the form of a white knight after he prayed for help due to Josephus' influence (Sommer I: 62-73). Her persuasion of her brother Seraphe to set aside his grievance with Evalach to fight on his side (Sommer I: 52) is also made adequate by divine intervention elicited by Evalach's prayers (Sommer I: 55-61). Sarrasinte's divine power to decide the contest between Evalach and Tholomer over the rule of Sarras is supplanted by Christ's.

In the *Arthurian Vulgate,* high-status women fall into one of three categories: those that possess temporal power through land ownership and followers but lack spiritual power, those that lack temporal power or neglect the duties of leadership and/or land ownership but use divine power in a Christian framework, and those that possess both temporal and supernatural power and are based on an adapted prechristian model. The questing lady Flegentine appropriates a masculine role to further support her husband, a feminine role, in a brief episode that is likely the product of one author and is closed with Flegentine having accomplished nothing by another author.

2 Gender and Metaphor

2.1 The False Queen and the Lion

Both the *Odyssey* and the *Arthurian Vulgate* are more likely to personify abstract ideas as female rather than male. Specifically, the two texts each engage with a female embodiment of the uncertainty of the correspondence between the signifier and the signified through a false queen story. In the *Arthurian Vulgate*, there are two Guineveres: the true one who is the daughter of king Leodagan and his wife, and the false one who was born of Leodagan and his seneschal's wife (Sommer II: 148-149). The sources of the *Vulgate* also contain multiple Guineveres: the Welsh Triads list three Guineveres as king Arthur's wife (RBH 15), and a blow from a Gwenhwyfach to Guinevere as a harmful blow in Britain (RBH 12). In the Welsh Triads, these three Guineveres are named as the wife of Arthur: Guinevere daughter of Cywryd Gwent, Guinevere daughter of Gwythyr son of Greidiawl, and Guinevere daughter of Gogfran the Giant (RBH 15). This suggests that multiplicity may be an aspect of Guinevere's character before the composition of the *Arthurian Vulgate*. None of these Guineveres is Guinevere daughter of Leodagan, who is both the True and the False Guinevere who appear in the

Arthurian Vulgate, suggesting that the Guineveres that appear in the

Arthurian Vulgate are recent additions to the material relative to those

named in the Welsh Triads.

Another possible correspondence between the Guineveres of the

oral sources summarized in the Welsh Triads and those that appear in the

later *Arthurian Vulgate* is between the Gwenhwyfach who hits Guinevere

(RBH 12) and the False Guinevere. In the triad of harmful blows of

Britain, a blow from Gwenhwyfach to Guinevere at court is listed; no

details of the conflict between them or its resolution are recounted,

leaving two possible women in the *Arthurian Vulgate* to be identified

with her: the False Guinevere, who challenged the True Guinevere at

court, and Morgan, who was exiled from court by Guinevere because she

had an adulterous affair with a young man at court. Neither of these

women have a name that can be identified as a translation or later form of

Gwenhwyfach[16], but both are attached to a story that may correspond to

---

[16] The name Gwenhwyfach and Guinevere, Gwenhwyfar in Welsh, do share the element Gwen-, white/shining, but they are distinct names because they are each compounded with a different second element which is of unclear etymology (Schrijver, 249-250). A variant etymology of Guinevere's name, suggesting that it may derive from Gwenhwy-fawr, or "Gwenhwy the Great", as a contrast to Gwenhwy-fach, or "Gwenhwy the less" supports the characters' distinctiveness. Melville Richards

the story that contained Gwenhwyfach's blow on Guinevere.

Gwenhwyfach is named as Guinevere's sister in the Mabinogion story of

Kilhwch and Olwen (Guest: 1877), which is also in the Red Book of

Hergest, which makes her slightly more likely to have entered the

Arthurian Vulgate as the False Guinevere, without ruling out the

possibility that the story of her and Guinevere's quarrel did not become

attached to Morgan and Guinevere later.

The historical sources are unhelpful in distinguishing which

Guinevere is the wife of king Arthur, since none of them names her

father. The lack of a named father for Guinevere in the Latin historical

sources obscures her connection to the Guineveres of the Welsh tradition;

Guinevere could have been given a father in the material based on the

Latin historical sources because these sources did not transmit

Guinevere's parentage.

The two Guineveres appear together in three places in the

Arthurian Vulgate: the story of their conception (Sommer II: 148-149),

---

(1969, p. 257) dismisses this etymology (suggesting that Gwenhwyfach
was a back-formation derived from an incorrect interpretation of
Gwenwhy-far as Gwenhwy-fawr).

the story of the false Guinevere's attempt to replace the true Guinevere with herself on her wedding night (Sommer II: 301-312), and the story of the false Guinevere coming to court to claim the throne as the true Guinevere. Each of these episodes contributes to the meaning of Guinevere as a character and in her roles in the *Arthurian Vulgate*, as well as the same of the other figures she shares these stories with. The false Guinevere stories were not all composed at the same time; they were added to the *Vulgate* in stages.

The story of the False Guinevere's claim to the throne is the oldest of the three stories. It is the story with the least rationalization because it lacks the distinguishing mark on either Guinevere of the stories of their conception and the attempted switch on the True Guinevere's wedding night and it contains the most recourse to divine intervention. It begins rationally, with the False Guinevere's messenger and cousin presenting her letter stating her claims to court with Bertalay the Old and a trial being arranged (Sommer IV: 10-17). The next episode of the story is the False Guinevere having Arthur kidnapped at Bertalay's advice, whom she subsequently keeps with her and drugs into falling in love with her and who names her queen while his court is left to assume that he has

died (Sommer IV: 44-51).

When he returns to court with the False Guinevere and Bertalay,

Arthur declares the False Guinevere to be the daughter of king Leodagan

and the true Guinevere to be the daughter of king Leodagan's seneschal,

Cleodalis (Sommer IV: 55). Bertolay, the False Guinevere, and the

barons of king Leodagan's kingdom, Carmelide, all swear that the False

Guinevere is the true one (Sommer IV: 55-56). Bertalay is the one who

decides that, since Guinevere's supporters have prevented Arthur from

putting Guinevere to death, she should be punished by having every part

of her body that came into contact with the sacrements of the queen cut

off and being permanently exiled (Sommer IV: 56-59).

The sentence is not carried out because Lancelot wins a trial by

combat as the True Guinevere's champion (Sommer IV: 60-67) and

Guinevere leaves to a gift of land from Galehaut with Arthur and the

False Guinevere's permission (Sommer IV: 68-69). With the land and the

status that came from it, the True Guinevere refused to ask Lancelot to

rejoin him after he had renounced his allegiance before participating in the trial by combat (Sommer IV: 71). Arthur has effectively severed his relationship with the True Guinevere in favour of supplanting her with the False Guinevere; the True Guinevere acts as if she were still married to Arthur, but Arthur acts as if he were not married to her.

The incident is resolved through divine means: the Pope interdicts Arthur's kingdom due to his adultery with the False Guinevere for twenty-one months, and in the eleventh month the False Guinevere and Bertelay the Old fall ill due to God's displeasure at the false queen and her kingmaker: they became paralyzed from the extremities up and then rot (Sommer IV: 72-73). Gawain takes Arthur hunting as an opportunity to convince him to give up the False Guinevere, and they end up eating in the True Guinevere's childhood confessor Amustans' house, where he lives as a hermit. Arthur becomes ill enough there to want the sacrament, which Amustans refuses to give him until he repents deserting his wife; Arthur recovers after he takes the sacrament (Sommer IV: 76-77). Amustans then elicits a confession from both the False Guinevere and Bertolay the Old (Sommer IV: 79-80). The True Guinevere then gives up her land in Sorlois and returns to Britain as the lawful wife of Arthur (Sommer IV: 82-83).

Divine intervention is the solution to the False Guinevere's

illegitimate holding of the True Guinevere's position: the Pope, God

directly through illness, and Amustans all distinguish between the True

and False Guineveres correctly and act to switch them back into their

proper roles. The secular interventions of the Barons of both Arthur and

Leodagan's kingdoms are either ineffective or on the wrong side

respectively. No matter how her husband treated her for love of the False

Guinevere, the True Guinevere is expected to behave the same way

towards him as before, since her treatment of her husband corresponds to

his treatment of God. The irony is, although those with access to God's

power can distinguish which Guinevere is the lawfully wedded wife and

sign of Arthur's legitimacy, both Guineveres are false in their loyalty to

Arthur: the False Guinevere represents herself as her sister, and the True

Guinevere has an adulterous affair (De Looze, 2014)[17].

The youngest of these three stories are the two stories of the

Guineveres' conception and of the False Guinevere's attempted

---

[17] This is also the source for the line of argument interpreting the False
Helen in this manner.

abduction and replacement with herself of the True Guinevere. The former's prerogative of rationalizing the two's differences and providing the True Guinevere who was almost abducted and replaced by her half-sister with a distinctive mark to prove her identity label the two stories as contemporary additions. Unlike the story of the False Guinevere's claim at court, these stories give a natural rather than supernatural method to distinguish the True and False Guineveres. The story of the substitution was expanded out of the False Guinevere's claims at court.

The False Guinevere's reliance on Bertelay the Red after she is exiled for the failure of her abduction and replacement plan invites a parallel to the True Guinevere and the king who offers to support her in the failure of her marriage to Arthur, Galehaut. Bertelay the Red is in this sense the False Galehaut to the False Guinevere. When he is introduced into the narrative before the attempted kidnapping story, it is through a story of failed courtly love that falls from a state that parallels the situation of Lancelot, Guinevere, and Arthur's relationships that ends in Bertelay being disinherited as a punishment for murder, having killed the lover of his wife who was also his cousin (Sommer II: 310-313). He is the same character as Bertolay the Old from the False Guinevere at court episode; their relationship is explained by his joining her in exile to revenge himself on king Arthur.

Bertelay the Red could be a False Arthur, since in the Welsh Triads Arthur is named as the red ravager of Britain who is worse than the three of the triad proper (RBH 23). Arthur is described in relation to the triad of ravagers as: "For a year neither grass nor plants used to spring up where one of the three would walk; but where Arthur went, not for seven years" (RBH 23). This exceptional bloodthirstiness is not directly attributed to Arthur beyond the original Welsh version of his character. In the Latin histories, king Arthur is not censured for excessive bloodthirstiness, and the *Arthurian Vulgate* generally follows their lead. The exception could be Arthur's insistence on fighting Mordred despite the knowledge that it will kill him (Sommer VI: 360-381), which may also be an artefact of the dissonance between the idealized Arthur that heads the round table and the less idealized Arthur in the Latin historical sources that set the manner of Arthur's death. It also calls to mind the possible results should Arthur discover his wife's infidelity.

A power of Guinevere as queen, namely her ability to give a measure of legitimacy to her husband's authority, is a focus of the tension in the False Guinevere at court episode. Since the True Guinevere is holy by virtue of her anointment as queen and gives her husband access to her inheritance of her father's kingdom, she holds the legitimacy of Arthur as an anointed king in general and his rule of king Leodagan's kingdom in particular. The accusation that he is not legitimately married to his wife and that he has introduced miasmic contamination to his people by living in adultery with a non-wife who had no right to be anointed as his queen or to grant him rule over the True Guinevere's inheritance is a serious challenge to Arthur's legitimacy as a king.

The condemnation of the False Guinevere for obtaining a husband through a false identity is in contrast to another false identity that is instrumental in a trick to secure a spouse: that of Uther Pendragon taking on the likeness of duke Gorlois in order to have sex with Igraine in the *Merlin Continuation* (Sommer II: 66-68). The story may be original to the Welsh material, since Uther Pendragon's illusion appears on a list of illusions of Britain (Peniarth MS 54, 25), but this identification is uncertain because the entry contains no explanation of what the illusion was. This supports the idea that a husband's treatment of his wife was not

a reflection of his attitude towards God as it is for a wife's treatment of

her husband; only his espousal of one woman, neither the deception by

which Uther Pendragon becomes the father of Arthur nor his choice not

to tell Igraine he was the father of her child (Sommer II: 73-74) counts

against him.

The False Helen does not appear as a character separate from

Argive Helen in the *Odyssey*. Since the *Odyssey* is concerned with oral

composition and what could undermine the signifier/signified

correspondence in a performed, not written, narrative, Helen's falseness

is internal to her character. In her appearance entertaining Telemachus

and Peisistratus in Menelaus' palace, Helen blocks the natural signs of

grief that Telemachus, Menelaus, and Helen herself shed at the uncertain

fate of Odysseus, and that Peisistratus shed for his dead brother

Antilochus, with the drug she mixed into the wine. Helen's act not only

cuts off the natural sign of tears from the group, but also falsifies

Menelaus' statement of how they will spend the feast:

ἡμεῖς δὲ κλαυθμὸν μὲν ἐάσομεν, ὃς πρὶν ἐτύχθη,

δόρπου δ᾽ ἐξαῦτις μνησώμεθα, χερσὶ δ᾽ ἐφ᾽ ὕδωρ

χευάντων. μῦθοι δὲ καὶ ἠῶθέν περ ἔσονται

Τηλεμάχῳ καὶ ἐμοὶ διαειπέμεν ἀλλήλοισιν. (4.212-215)

But we will cease the weeping which but now was made, and let

us once more think of our supper, and let them pour water over

our hands. Tales there will be in the morning also for Telemachus

and me to tell to one another to the full. (Murray 1919)

This speech, performed by the host of the feast, should signify that in the

morning after the feast was over the conversation will turn back to what

had made them cry. Helen's drug, however, prevents this from

happening.

αὐτίκ᾽ ἄρ᾽ εἰς οἶνον βάλε φάρμακον, ἔνθεν ἔπινον,

νηπενθές τ᾽ ἄχολόν τε, κακῶν ἐπίληθον ἁπάντων.

ὃς τὸ καταβρόξειεν, ἐπὴν κρητῆρι μιγείη,

οὔ κεν ἐφημέριός γε βάλοι κατὰ δάκρυ παρειῶν,

οὐδ᾽ εἴ οἱ κατατεθναίη μήτηρ τε πατήρ τε,

οὐδ᾽ εἴ οἱ προπάροιθεν ἀδελφεὸν ἢ φίλον υἱὸν

χαλκῷ δηιόῳεν, ὁ δ᾽ ὀφθαλμοῖσιν ὁρῷτο. (4.221-226)

Straightway she cast into the wine of which they were drinking a

drug to quiet all pain and strife, and bring forgetfulness of every

ill. Whoso should drink this down, when it is mingled in the bowl, would not in the course of that day let a tear fall down over his

cheeks, no, not though his mother and father should lie there dead,

or though before his face men should slay with the sword his

brother or dear son, and his own eyes beheld it. (Murray 1919)

Helen's use of this drug disconnects the performance of the stories that

will actually be told after the feast from the emotion behind them. Unlike

Circe's use of drugs, Helen's does not stem from her own skill or effort.

She is given the one she uses from a character that only appears in the

Odyssey, Polydamna, which means tamer of many; as befits her sole

appearance, her name describes what she does through her drugs. Helen's

action, administrating the drug, cuts their narrative (sign) off from its

content (signified). Another aspect of these passages is that they place

Odysseus on the same level as several definitely deceased figures:

Antilochus and the close relatives listed in the description of the drug's

effects. Since Odysseus is still with Calypso at this point in the story, this

implication of Odysseus' death fits with his stay on Ogygia being a stay

in the underworld.

Under the influence of the drug, both Helen and Menelaus tell a

story of Odysseus' heroics. Helen tells of how Odysseus disguised himself as a beggar to get into Troy unopposed and her own collusion with him after she saw through how Odysseus had "αὐτόν μιν πληγῇσιν ἀεικελίῃσι δαμάσσας, / σπεῖρα κάκ' ἀμφ' ὤμοισι βαλών, οἰκῆι ἐοικώς, / ἀνδρῶν δυσμενέων κατέδυ πόλιν εὐρυάγυιαν" (4.244-246), "himself he conquered with unseemly blows, / throwing poor cloaks over both shoulders, appearing like a slave, / he went down the wide city streets of hostile men". Helen sees through the marks Odysseus put on his body that were meant to show him as a menial slave to be ignored and marks him as himself. Helen goes on to keep Odysseus' identity secret from the Trojans, allowing him to kill many of them and bring back secrets to the Achaean camp. Helen facilitates Odysseus' false identity, splitting his outer presentation (signifier) from his identity (signified).

Helen also presents a false version of herself in this story, since in the aftermath of Odysseus' killing spree she was there when:

ἔνθ' ἄλλαι Τρωαὶ λίγ' ἐκώκυον: αὐτὰρ ἐμὸν κῆρ

χαῖρ', ἐπεὶ ἤδη μοι κραδίη τέτραπτο νέεσθαι

ἂψ οἶκόνδ', ἄτην δὲ μετέστενον, ἣν Ἀφροδίτη

δῶχ', ὅτε μ' ἤγαγε κεῖσε φίλης ἀπὸ πατρίδος αἴης,

παῖδά τ' ἐμὴν νοσφισσαμένην θάλαμόν τε πόσιν τε

οὔ τευ δευόμενον, οὔτ᾽ ἄρ φρένας οὔτε τι εἶδος. (4.259-264)

Then the other Trojan women wailed aloud, but my soul was glad,

for already my heart was turned to go back to my home, and I

groaned for the blindness that Aphrodite gave me, when she led

me thither from my dear native land, forsaking my child and my

bridal chamber, and my husband, a man who lacked nothing,

whether in wisdom or in comeliness. (Murray 1919)

Helen counts herself among the Trojan women in the first line of this

sentence, but she immediately separates herself from the group through

her true feelings. She does not mourn alongside the Trojans, as she did

not show any loyalty to them when presented with the opportunity to out

Odysseus. This entire story can be seen as Helen telling her husband and

guests, who are all linked to the Achaean side of the war, that she

considers going to Troy a mistake, a folly caused by Aphrodite, and that

she was really on their side. In effect, to the end of presenting herself in a

more positive light to her audience, Helen is arguing that the version of

herself that left for Troy was a false one.

The story Menelaus tells of Odysseus also comments on Helen; it

has her test Odysseus and the others in the Trojan horse. She walks around the Trojan horse followed by her second Trojan husband, Deiphobus, and knocks on it to discover that it is hollow. Helen then proceeds to imitate the voices of the Achaean chiefs' wives to tempt them to respond and give away their ambush, an effort which Odysseus blocks by restraining his fellows in the horse. Meneleus attributes her actions to divine influence, saying that she approached the Trojan horse, "ἦλθες ἔπειτα σὺ κεῖσε: κελευσέμεναι δέ σ' ἔμελλε / δαίμων, ὃς Τρώεσσιν ἐβούλετο κῦδος ὀρέξαι" (4.274-275), "you then went there: you were about to be urged by a divine power, who was willing to extend renown to the Trojans".

The description of why Helen decided to test the Trojan horse is vague and ambiguous: Menelaus does not name which deity is involved, and only indirectly states that Helen tests the Danaans by imitating their wives' voices because some divine power ordered her. Helen's own divine power is conveniently not mentioned. If Helen had been the deity responsible for her urge to test the horse, then she would have willingly chosen to help the Trojans win renown during the Trojan War instead of having been passively affected by outer influences to do the same. By disconnecting Helen's actions from her capacity to act under her own willpower, Menelaus distances her from the blame that would fall on her

if she acted against the Greeks intentionally. Once again, the Helen who

left for Troy is made false.

The way Menelaus describes Helen giving up on trying to induce

the Greeks in the horse to give themselves away as, "σε νόσφιν ἀπήγαγε

Παλλὰς Ἀθήνη" (4.289), "Pallas Athena led you away". This action fits

Athena's ongoing role as Odysseus' divine protector, and Odysseus'

action in silencing the other men in the horse fits his ongoing role as a

hero distinguished by his restraint. Once again Helen does not act of her

own free will, but is led to act by a divine influence. However, in contrast

to the divine explanation for her beginning the test, the influence to lead

her away is named as acting directly on Helen and makes sense with the

rest of the story. Taken together, the two ends of Menelaus' story show

him taking pains to avoid blaming Helen for taking the Trojan side in the

Trojan War with the same tactic as Helen herself, reducing her agency.

These two stories each praise Odysseus for his heroics in the

context of an interaction with Helen that also displays her heroic

qualities. The drug Helen added into the kraton disconnected these stories from the feeling or memory of pain or anger, which as well as damping

any grief over Odysseus, greatly impacted how the issue of Helen's

unclear loyalties during the Trojan War was handled during the

performance of each story. Since all of the participants of this

performance other than Helen belong to the Greek side of the war, and

have either lost close family members like Peisistratus lost his brother

Antilochus or Telemachus had presumably lost Odysseus or experienced

the hardships of the war firsthand like Menelaus, recounting stories that

show how Helen's loyalties were split by her ties to both sides would

likely bring up both grief and anger in them that could be directed at

Helen as a Trojan supporter. With the emotion from their experiences in

the Trojan War gone from themselves and their audience, the possibility

of them attaching or reinforcing a negative opinion of Helen or Odysseus

by association with the experience of hearing or telling the stories is cut

off. In the absence of this true emotional influence, both Helen and

Menelaus focus on promoting Helen's current and suspect loyalty to her

return to the status quo ante bellum.

In service of this slant to their stories, both Helen and Menelaus

seek to undermine the truth of the Helen who went to Troy; the true

Helen is the one who is loyal to her spouse, child, and homeland, any of her actions that act against this Helen are explained away as the result of another's will. The true meaning of the stories that the drug cuts them off from is that they are evidence of a Helen with divided loyalties which she could not reconcile enough to support both at once, and therefore vacillated between each. In Helen's story, she acted like she was on the Greek side; in Menelaus', she acted like she was on the Trojan side. A connection to the emotions embedded in the memories that these stories recollect would have made the connection between Helen's actions and unsure loyalty apparent, but the disconnection allowed the two of them to build a false version of events that suits their reconciliation. The false Helen built by this exercise is the one who did not choose to become a Trojan woman, but was instead manipulated by divine intervention to perform actions she would herself regret. At no point is Helen actually split into two figures, only rhetorically.

There are, however, several false Helens that exist independently of the original Argive Helen in non-epic workings of the Trojan Cycle material written after the composition of the *Odyssey*. She arises out of contexts where a bias towards Argive Helen is appropriate, initially

choral poetry associated with the localized worship of Helen as a
goddess, and later exercises of rhetorical prowess. There are three
different false Helens presented in three sources: Stesichorus' Helen as
summarized in Dio Chrysostom, a section of Herodotus' *Histories*, and
the *Helen* of Euripides.

These stories all agree with the tradition that Helen spent some
time in Egypt around the time of the Trojan War, and use it to put their
true Helen out of the way while the false Helen is at Troy. In the
Odyssey, Menelaus and Helen and stop in Egypt on the way back from
Helen's recovery from Troy, where they are becalmed on Pharos by
divine displeasure and Menelaus finds the solution to get home from,
"γέρων ἅλιος νημερτὴς / ἀθάνατος Πρωτεὺς Αἰγύπτιος, ὅς τε θαλάσσης /
πάσης βένθεα οἶδε," (4.384-6), "the unerring old man of the sea /
immortal Proteus the Egyptian, who of the sea / knows all the depths".
Menelaus' experience obtaining this prophetic aid from Proteus with the
instruction of his daughter Eidothea is a parallel to Odysseus obtaining
prophetic aid from Tiresias so that he can overcome the divine
displeasure of Poseidon and get home after Circe tells him how.

This story in the *Odyssey* contains germs of the themes that will

be expanded upon in the later sources with a false Helen: Eidothea

(Εἰδοθέη) is the goddess of visible form (εἰδός), which is what the word

for Helen's false double, εἴδωλον, is derived from and Proteus defends

himself from being forced to prophecy for Menelaus by "πάντα δὲ

γιγνόμενος" (4.417), "becoming everything", a polysemousness which is

later exploited in rhetorical defences to reinterpret the elements of

Helen's character. These broad concepts of the feminine visible form and

defensive transformation present in the *Odyssey*'s version of Helen's time

in Egypt will be repurposed for the later false Helen stories.

Little of Stesichorus' works are extant. He wrote slightly later that

the composition of the *Odyssey*, both in praise and in blame of Helen,

which only exists in summary by Dio Chrysostom in his eleventh

discourse. The argument of Dio's eleventh discourse is that Homer's

poetry is deceptive of the facts of what happened during the Trojan War,

and in the service of this thesis he brings in a summary of Stesichorus'

writing in favour of Helen. The first story he includes is about

Stesichorus himself:

ποιητὴν ἕτερον Ὁμήρῳ πεισθέντα καὶ ταὐτὰ πάντα ποιήσαντα περὶ

Ἑλένης, Στησίχορον, ὡς οἶμαι, τυφλωθῆναί φατε ὑπὸ τῆς Ἑλένης,

ὡς ψευσάμενον, αὖθις δὲ ἀναβλέψαι τἀναντία ποιήσαντα. (D.Chr.

11.40)

Another poet — Stesichorus, I believe it is — who followed

Homer's account and repeated these same stories about Helen, that

he was struck blind by her as a liar and recovered his sight upon

recanting. (Cohoon 1932)

Implicit in this description is that the power to take and give back a

person's sight is proper to a deity; the Helen who takes away Stesichorus'

sight is the same Helen who is worshipped as a goddess in Lacedonia. It

also shows the false Helen of Homer, who is mortal, be replaced by the

true Helen of cult in the work of the poet.

The story of Stesichorus' sight is not the invention of Dio, since it

also appears in a form that suggests it is older than Dio's version in

Pausanias' *Description of Greece*. In Pausanias, the wounded king

Leonymus is told by the prophetess at Delphi that he may be cured by

Ajax son of Oileus, who wounded him, on the White Island (Paus.

3.19.12). On the island, Leonymus sees Achilles with the two Ajaxes,

Patroclus and Antilochus as well as:

> Ἑλένην δὲ Ἀχιλλεῖ μὲν συνοικεῖν, προστάξαι δέ οἱ πλεύσαντι ἐς
>
> Ἱμέραν πρὸς Στησίχορον ἀγγέλλειν ὡς ἡ διαφθορὰ τῶν ὀφθαλμῶν
>
> ἐξ Ἑλένης γένοιτο αὐτῷ μηνίματος. Στησίχορος μὲν ἐπὶ τούτῳ τὴν
>
> παλινῳδίαν ἐποίησεν (Paus. 3.19.13).

> Helen was wedded to Achilles, and had bidden him sail to
>
> Stesichorus at Himera, and announce that the loss of his sight was
>
> caused by her wrath. Therefore Stesichorus composed his
>
> recantation. (Jones & Ormerod 1918)

Not only Helen, but also Achilles and the other heroes of the Greek side

of the Trojan War have a divine presence on the White Island. This story

takes place after Achilles, Patroclus, and Antilochus had died during the

Trojan War and when Ajax son of Oileus had already settled in Italy after

the war. These doubles of the dead or present elsewhere heroes are their

characters' superhuman elements, which are immortal, cut off from their

mortal humanity.

It efficiently resolves the ontological split of a Greek hero

between their divine and mortal elements, like the story of Heracles' death and apotheosis. In the Nekyia, Odysseus encounters Heracles, "τὸν

δὲ μετ᾽ εἰσενόησα βίην Ἡρακληείην, / εἴδωλον· αὐτὸς δὲ μετ᾽ ἀθανάτοισι

θεοῖσι" (*Od* 11.601-602), "then I [Odysseus] saw mighty Heracles among

them / a phantom: himself was among the immortal gods". The Heracles

who is immortal due to his father Zeus abides among the gods, the

phantom (εἴδωλον) of his human half from his mother Alcmene abides

among the dead in Hades.

Dio quotes from what he calls only "τῇ ὕστερον ᾠδῇ" (11.41),

"the last Ode". It is implied but not stated that this is the recantation

mentioned in Pausanias and the writing opposite to Homer mentioned

earlier in the same discourse. Stesichorus through Dio asserts that Helen

is blameless for the Trojan War because "οὐδὲ πλεύσειεν ἡ Ἑλένη

οὐδαμόσε" (11.41), "Helen did not sail anywhere". Dio then goes into

details that Stesichorus' work in turn quotes from an Egyptian priest for

the truth of the story, since: "τοῖς μὲν ποιηταῖς ἐπιτρέπουσιν, ὅτι ἂν

θέλωσι ψεύδεσθαι καί φασιν ἐξεῖναι αὐτοῖς, ὅμως δὲ πιστεύουσινοῖς ἂν

ἐκεῖνοι λέγωσι" (11.42), "They [Greeks] turn to the poets, who would

want to beguile and say it is allowed to them, nevertheless they would

trust what these people say", and "ἡ δὲ ποίησις ἀναπείθει τὰ ψευδῆ ἀκούειν ὥσπερ ὁ οἶνος πίνειν μάτην" (11.43), "poetry convinces people

to listen to lies like wine does to drink to madness". The argument that

this leads to is that the Helen of epic poetry is false because poets lie.

Stesichorus through Dio explains that Helen went to Troy as Paris'

legitimately betrothed bride, and that the Greeks besieged Troy in order

to gain booty and assert themselves over barbarian foreigners. Dio

undertakes this discourse with a similar motivation, to assert himself the

rhetorician over Homer the poet.

Herodotus recounts a story that a priest at the temple of 'Foreign

Aphrodite', whom Herodotus interprets as the name the Egyptians use to

worship Helen, told him about Helen (Hdt. 2.112-119). On the way to

Troy with Helen and treasure from Menelaus' palace, Paris is sent off

course to Egypt by bad weather. The high priest of the temple of 'Foreign

Aphrodite' discovers that Paris has stolen the treasure and wife of his

guest-friend and reports it to the pharaoh, Proteus, who forces Paris to

leave Egypt without Helen and the treasure from Menelaus. When

Menelaus and the other Greeks reach Troy to take Helen and the treasure

back, the Trojans tell them that what they want is in Egypt. However,

expecting that the Trojans were mocking them, "Ἕλληνες καταγελᾶσθαι δοκέοντες" (2.118.4), the Greeks did not believe that Helen and the

treasure were not at Troy, and besieged the city. After the city was taken

Menelaus went to Egypt and got Helen and his treasure back.

Herodotus adds that he finds this account convincing, because "εἰ

ἦν Ἑλένη ἐν Ἰλίῳ, ἀποδοθῆναι ἂν αὐτὴν τοῖσι Ἕλλησι ἤτοι ἑκόντος γε ἢ

ἀέκοντος Ἀλεξάνδρου" (2.120.1), "if Helen were in Ilium, she really

would have been handed over to the Greeks whether Alexandros [Paris]

was willing or unwilling". He goes on to rationalize why continuing to go

to war over keeping Helen and Menelaus' treasure despite many of his

sons dying for them makes no sense for Priam, and therefore Priam must

have been unable to hand them over. Herodotus' account essentially

eliminates the supernatural elements of the existing stories that place

Helen in Egypt around the time of the Trojan War. Proteus is a human

pharaoh, not the superhuman old man of the sea; there is no Helen

εἴδωλον, only the false belief that Helen was at Troy. Menelaus and the

rest of the Greeks misinterpret the Trojans' story as a lie, and this false

reading in effect creates a false Helen who arrived at Troy with Paris.

The real Helen, or the true interpretation of the Trojans' speech, is where

the Trojans said she/it was.

Euripides' *Helen* actually uses a story that has Helen be replaced

by an εἴδωλον, who goes to Troy instead of Helen herself. In the

prologue, Helen explains how this came about from the tomb of the

pharaoh Proteus in Egypt, beginning with the judgment of Paris:

Κύπρις προτείνασ᾽ ὡς Ἀλέξανδρος γαμεῖ,

νικᾷ. λιπὼν δὲ βούσταθμ᾽ Ἰδαῖος Πάρις

Σπάρτην ἀφίκεθ᾽ ὡς ἐμὸν σχήσων λέχος.

Ἥρα δὲ μεμφθεῖσ᾽ οὕνεκ᾽ οὐ νικᾷ θεάς,

ἐξηνέμωσε τἄμ᾽ Ἀλεξάνδρῳ λέχη,

δίδωσι δ᾽ οὐκ ἔμ᾽, ἀλλ᾽ ὁμοιώσασ᾽ ἐμοὶ

εἴδωλον ἔμπνουν οὐρανοῦ ξυνθεῖσ᾽ ἄπο,

Πριάμου τυράννου παιδί: καὶ δοκεῖ μ᾽ ἔχειν,

κενὴν δόκησιν, οὐκ ἔχων. (28-36)

Kypris offered my beauty, if misfortune is beautiful, for Paris to

marry, and so she won. Paris, the shepherd of Ida, left his ox-stalls

and came to Sparta, to have me in marriage. But Hera, indignant

at not defeating the goddesses, made an airy nothing of my

marriage with Paris; she gave to the son of king Priam not me, but

an image, alive and breathing, that she fashioned out of the sky and made to look like me; and he thinks he has me—an idle

fancy, for he doesn't have me. (Oates & O'Neil 1938)

This excerpt is the oldest extant source of the explanation of how Helen

did not cause the Trojan War because she had been replaced by an

εἴδωλον of herself. The further details of the story serve to set up her safe

retrieval by Menelaus as he returns from Troy. Helen is protected by

Proteus the pharaoh during the Trojan War, and Menelaus is conveniently

shipwrecked onto Egypt after Proteus dies and Helen loses his protection.

The εἴδωλον even explains Helen's innocence before having to "πατέρ'

ἐς οὐρανὸν ἄπειμι" (Eur *Hel* 613-614), "go away into the sky my father"

because her work was done.

      Hera's creation of the Helen εἴδωλον out of a cloud by Hera in

Euripides is likely inspired by Zeus' creation of a Hera εἴδωλον to test

Ixion's respect for his hospitality. The Hera εἴδωλον is first attested to in

Pindar's Pythian 2, when it is invoked in a list of stories that involve the

guest/host relationship. Ixion, the guest of Zeus, conceives an

inappropriate lust for his host's wife, which is satisfied:

     νεφέλᾳ παρελέξατο,

     ψεῦδος γλυκὺ μεθέπων, ἄϊδρις ἀνήρ:

εἶδος γὰρ ὑπεροχωτάτᾳ πρέπεν οὐρανιᾶν

θυγατέρι Κρόνου (36-39)

the man in his ignorance chased a sweet fake and lay with a cloud,

for its form was like the supreme celestial goddess, the daughter

of Cronus. (Svarlien 1990)

This description of the false Hera uses the related word for image, εἶδος,

and the word for cloud, νεφέλᾳ, to refer to the false Hera used as a decoy

in this story, never εἴδωλον. The false Hera survives this episode as a

separate character from Hera, and later tradition preserved in the libraries

of Apollodorus (1.9) and Siculus (4.12), and in Hyginus' *Astronomica*

(2.20), use the common word for cloud (Νεφέλη in Greek, Nubis in

Latin) as her name. Within the ode, Pindar gives the story its purpose by

how he begins and ends it: the section of his ode devoted to this story is

bookended by Pindar naming Ixion's punishment for having sex with

what he thought was Hera as a warning to any mortal who would violate

hospitality.

Euripides, when he appropriated the story of Nephele and applied

it to his play, which demanded a pro-Helen angle, also included the

thematic concerns that were attached to it in Pindar's version. Like

Nephele, the Helen εἴδωλον is created to absorb an attack on the chastity of the wife she was made to resemble; in both the play and the ode, the original of the image is under immanent threat, Hera by Ixion and Helen by Paris, a threat which is renewed in the action of Euripides' *Helen* by Proteus' heir. Both Helen and Menelaus need to call on the hospitality of Proteus, Helen both when he was alive and at his tomb, and Menelaus only the latter; the threat to Helen by Proteus' heir, namely to replace her husband, is the same one presented by Ixion to Hera. In effect, Euripides added the elements of a story about Hera avoiding rape with a duplicate made of a cloud to the tradition of asserting that Helen was blameless for the Trojan War and the traditional solution of splitting figures considered both human and divine into a human εἴδωλον and a divine true self to resolve the figure's internal contradictions. Of these three elements, only the first is original to Euripides.

The Helen εἴδωλον in Euripedes most closely resembles the false Guinevere in the *Arthurian Vulgate*. She appears as both the externalization of Helen's role opening a disconnect between a sign and its meaning and an internalization of the same into Helen's character. The false queen story in the *Arthurian Vulgate* is much more developed than the one in the *Odyssey*; the divine elements attributed to Guinevere's character as a queen have already been sublimated into her queenship rather than settled into her person in the *Arthurian Vulgate*, where in the *Odyssey* Helen's divinity is a part of her character emphasized in contexts other than epic poetry. The *Arthurian Vulgate* also shows more development of this story in that it has subsumed the origin of the False Guinevere as a tool for explaining away the contradictions of her character into an extended metaphor of two different Guineveres, one of whom is completely true to her husband and her other obligations as queen, and one of whom is completely antithetical to the same responsibilities.

Both versions of the false queen story seek to resolve ontological as well as moral ambiguity in the queen's character by splitting her into two versions of herself. Helen and Guinevere have a history of being considered goddess in some contexts; Helen's local worship was not transmitted to her role in the Panhellenic Homeric poems, and Guinevere features in the role held by a goddess in cognates to several of her stories. Guinevere's worship, or the worship that was attracted to Guinevere by analogy with the class of divine queens through her role, was incompatible with Christianity and likely no longer practiced in Wales when she was introduced to a wide audience in the *Arthurian Vulgate*'s historical sources, so her divinity is only a vestige of her history left implicit in some of her stories.

The evidence available in the present is insufficient to discern whether Guinevere was originally worshipped as a goddess or a non-divine substitute that had taken the roles of the original goddess so the newly Christian Welsh could bring their mythology into line with their new religion. In either case, the *Arthurian Vulgate* reinterprets Guinevere's choices of lover, which would have been her prerogative in the role of a goddess, by the standards of morality that belonged to a mortal queen, which both the true and the false Guinevere fail to meet.

The *Odyssey* and the *Arthurian Vulgate* also both use the lion as a symbol. The *Arthurian Vulgate* draws on two sources of lion symbolism: the Bible and classical authors in Latin. The Bible uses the lion as a symbol in various contexts. One story that draws on the symbolism associated with this animal is Ezekiel 19. It uses the lion as a symbol representing a warrior on the side of the faithful. Like the story of

Samson's confrontation with a lion in the Timnathian vinyards at Judges 14, it uses the lion as a double for a person[18]. Ezekiel 19 is a lament for the nation of Israel. The nation in her former strength is personified first as a lioness, mother to the lion princes of Israel, then as a vine. The prophet Ezekiel addresses his audience:

> Et tu assume planctum super principes Israël, et dices: Quare mater tua leæna inter leones cubavit? in medio leunculorum enutrivit catulos suos? Et eduxit unum de leunculis suis, et leo factus est: et didicit capere prædam, hominemque comedere. Et audierunt de eo gentes: et non absque vulneribus suis ceperunt eum, et adduxerunt eum in catenis in terram Ægypti. (Ezekiel 19.1-4)

> Moreover take thou up a lamentation for the princes of Israel, And say, What is thy mother? A lioness: she lay down among lions, she nourished her whelps among young lions. And she brought up one of her whelps: it became a young lion, and it learned to catch the prey; it devoured men. The nations also heard of him; he was

---

[18] Samson is attacked by and kills a lion of his same status; like Samson, the lion is young, male, and searching for the means to reproduce (Strawn 2009).

taken in their pit, and they brought him with chains unto the land

of Egypt.

Israel as a lioness interacts with the princes as lions as an equal; she has

cubs with them, who leave as her princes. In this metaphor, Israel is a

lioness in name and an aristocratic woman in action. She has children

with fathers of her own class, who leave to engage in warfare with

plunder as an incentive.

When the narrative turns to the transition to Israel's weakness, the

metaphorical image of her changes from a lioness to a vine:

> Et factæ sunt ei virgæ solidæ in sceptra dominantium, et exaltata
>
> est statura ejus inter frondes, et vidit altitudinem suam in
>
> multitudine palmitum suorum. Et evulsa est in ira, in terramque
>
> projecta, et ventus urens siccavit fructum ejus: marcuerunt et
>
> arefactæ sunt virgæ roboris ejus: ignis comedit eam. Et nunc
>
> transplantata est in desertum, in terra invia et sitienti. Et egressus
>
> est ignis de virga ramorum ejus, qui fructum ejus comedit: et non
>
> fuit in ea virga fortis, sceptrum dominantium. Planctus est, et erit
>
> in planctum. (Ezekiel 19.11-14)

And she had strong rods for the scepters of them that bore rule,
and her stature was exalted among the thick branches, and she
appeared in her height with the multitude of her branches. But she
was plucked up in fury, she was cast down to the ground, and the
east wind dried up her fruit: her strong rods were broken and
withered; the fire consumed them. And now she is planted in the
wilderness, in a dry and thirsty ground. And fire is gone out of a
rod of her branches, which hath devoured her fruit, so that she
hath no strong rod to be a scepter to rule. This is a lamentation,
and shall be for a lamentation.

Both metaphors cast the nation as the mother of her princes, whether she
is a lioness and they are her cubs or she is a vine and they her offshoots.
The difference is in the amount of agency the nation of Israel has over
her state: Israel the lioness, despite the misfortune of her sons, remains
untouched herself and capable of persevering to have a successful one;
Israel the vine does not enjoy this independence, when her offshoots
suffer, she does, and she is doomed to suffer the effects of the weather
and the unattributed agent who moved her to the desert. Since the

weather is attributed to divine action[19] and God's agency is not directly blamed for misfortune in contexts where the story's purpose is not to assert divine justice[20], the one who causes Israel's suffering must be God. Israel's is powerless against the influence of God, as shown in the vine metaphor, but may contest against the other nations as an equal, as shown in the lion metaphor.

The classical sources available in Latin, as well as the New Testament, draw their uses of the lion as a symbol from the use of lions in Homeric similes in Greek. Lions are often the point of comparison to the character in these extended poetic comparisons, and like in the Old Testament, the lion is a symbol for members of the aristocratic warrior class. Both Odysseus and Penelope are compared to a lion in the *Odyssey*. Odysseus is compared to a lion when he overcomes his shame at his nudity to speak to Nausicaa and when Menelaus predicts that he will slaughter the suitors.

---

[19] Examples include: "By his [God's] knowledge the depths are broken up, and the clouds drop down the dew" (Proverbs 3.20), and in Job's praise of God's powers (Job 18.24-28).
[20] Examples include: Racheal's death in childbirth in Genesis (35.18), and the bet which had Satan inflicting suffering upon Job with God's permission rather than God inflict unjust suffering upon Job (Job 1.6-12).

He is compared as a lion towards the suitors in this simile spoken

by Menelaus to Telemachus:

ὡς δ᾽ ὁπότ᾽ ἐν ξυλόχῳ ἔλαφος κρατεροῖο λέοντος

νεβροὺς κοιμήσασα νεηγενέας γαλαθηνοὺς

κνημοὺς ἐξερέῃσι καὶ ἄγκεα ποιήεντα

βοσκομένη, ὁ δ᾽ ἔπειτα ἑὴν εἰσήλυθεν εὐνήν,

ἀμφοτέροισι δὲ τοῖσιν ἀεικέα πότμον ἐφῆκεν,

ὣς Ὀδυσεὺς κείνοισιν ἀεικέα πότμον ἐφήσει. (4.335-340)

Even as when in the thicket-lair of a mighty lion a hind has laid to

sleep her new-born suckling fawns, and roams over the mountain

slopes and grassy vales seeking pasture, and then the lion comes

to his lair and upon the two lets loose a cruel doom, so will

Odysseus let loose a cruel doom upon these men. (Murray 1919)

This simile is a hint at Odysseus' martial prowess, which will come to

bear when he finally defeats the suitors in his hall. It is also typical of the

lion similes in the *Iliad* that compare the prowess of a warrior to a lion

and logically fits with the use of the lion as a metaphorical representation

of a prince in the Old Testament. Since there were no lions in Greece in any period that could affect these similes, the symbolism of the lion must be an import from the Near East.

When he leaves the bushes to speak to Nausicaa, Odysseus is described with this simile:

βῆ δ' ἴμεν ὥς τε λέων ὀρεσίτροφος ἀλκὶ πεποιθώς,

ὅς τ' εἶσ' ὑόμενος καὶ ἀήμενος, ἐν δέ οἱ ὄσσε

δαίεται· αὐτὰρ ὁ βουσὶ μετέρχεται ἢ ὀίεσσιν

ἠὲ μετ' ἀγροτέρας ἐλάφους· κέλεται δέ ἑ γαστὴρ

μήλων πειρήσοντα καὶ ἐς πυκινὸν δόμον ἐλθεῖν·

ὣς Ὀδυσεὺς κούρῃσιν ἐυπλοκάμοισιν ἔμελλε

μίξεσθαι, γυμνός περ ἐών· χρειὼ γὰρ ἵκανε. (6.130-136)

Forth he came like a mountain-nurtured lion trusting in his might, who goes forth, beaten with rain and wind, but his two eyes are ablaze: into the midst of the kine he goes, or of the sheep, or on the track of the wild deer, and his belly bids him go even into the close-built fold, to make an attack upon the flocks. [135] Even so Odysseus was about to enter the company of the fair-tressed maidens, naked though he was, for need had come upon him. (Murray 1919)

Odysseus is compared to a lion in his moment of decision to go ahead

and speak to the girls. The choice of a predatory object of comparison fits

with the verb used for Odysseus joining the girls, μίξεσθαι. It can be used

to form sexual innuendoes that translate literally into English as: they

mingled together or similar formulations; Odysseus' nudity reinforces the

threat of inappropriate sexual contact. This helps cast Nausicaa's staying

to speak to Odysseus as brave, and her maids' flight as reasonable.

Penelope is a lion in this simile when she is kept awake worried

about the Suitors' plot on Telemachus' life: "ὅσσα δὲ μερμήριξε λέων

ἀνδρῶν ἐν ὁμίλῳ" (4.791), "she was in doubt as great as a lion in a crowd

of men". She is like a male lion, not a lioness like in the example from

the Old Testament above. This sets up an analogy with Odysseus' lion

simile in the Phaeacian episode: the strength of Odysseus' resolve was as

a hungry lion attacking food; the strength of Penelope's indecision is also

as strong as a lion about to attack. The lack of biological accuracy, which

is present in the Old Testament (Strawn 2009), points to both the lion

symbolism's status as an import from the Near East and not an extended

meaning drawn from an animal the society of the *Odyssey*'s composers

were directly aware of and to a parallel across the gender barrier between

Penelope and Odysseus. Penelope, like Odysseus, is compared to a lion; her static indecision and Odysseus' mobile decision are both equally worthy actions for a woman or man respectively in their positions.

Odysseus is compared to a member of the opposite gender in a simile in turn when he cries "ὡς δὲ γυνὴ κλαίῃσι φίλον πόσιν ἀμφιπεσοῦσα, / ὅς τε ἑῆς πρόσθεν πόλιος λαῶν τε πέσῃσιν, / ἄστεϊ καὶ τεκέεσσιν ἀμύνων νηλεὲς ἦμαρ" (8.523-525), "like a woman crying while embracing her beloved spouse, / who standing before his city fell from the army, / and died keeping the pitiless day off the town" at Demodocus' narration of the story of the Trojan horse. The city in the simile, like the city in Demodocus' song, falls and the woman is carried off a slave. It is this fit of weeping that attracts king Alcinous' questions about Odysseus' identity, which Odysseus answers with his narration of his adventures that led him to Scheria. Odysseus and Penelope's gender-switching similes invite the audience to consider the two of them equals, and by extension both the male and the female genders that they represent.

In the New Testament, the lion has switched sides from the Old

Testament: from representing the faithful warrior to representing the

enemy of the faithful, which is succinctly put in this admonition: "Sobrii

estote, et vigilate: quia adversarius vester diabolus tamquam leo rugiens

circuit, quærens quem devoret" (1 Peter 5.8), "Be sober, and vigilant:

because your adversary the devil as a lion circles roaring, asking whom

he will devour". This change can be attributed to the different attitudes

towards the warfare for plunder from which the class of people

represented by lions profited embedded in these two places in the Bible.

As such, lion similes and metaphors are essentially masculine, only being

attached to female characters through their relation to a gendered male

warrior. Since both the supportive and condemnatory symbolic meanings

were accessible in Latin, the authors of the *Arthurian Vulgate* were free

to draw from both to make symbolic statements.

2.2 The *Odyssey*

The rooted bedpost that appears in Penelope's test of Odysseus' identity at *Odyssey* 23, 174-205 not only represents Athena's support for the reintegration of Odysseus and Penelope's marriage but also a survival of the worship of gods through various nonfigural representations (stones, trees, pillars) from the Bronze Age. Odysseus describes how he built the bed himself in detail:

θάμνος ἔφυ τανύφυλλος ἐλαίης ἔρκεος ἐντός,

ἀκμηνὸς θαλέθων: πάχετος δ᾽ ἦν ἠΰτε κίων.

τῷ δ᾽ ἐγὼ ἀμφιβαλὼν θάλαμον δέμον, ὄφρ᾽ ἐτέλεσσα,

πυκνῇσιν λιθάδεσσι, καὶ εὖ καθύπερθεν ἔρεψα,

κολλητὰς δ᾽ ἐπέθηκα θύρας, πυκινῶς ἀραρυίας.

καὶ τότ᾽ ἔπειτ᾽ ἀπέκοψα κόμην τανυφύλλου ἐλαίης,

κορμὸν δ᾽ ἐκ ῥίζης προταμὼν ἀμφέξεσα χαλκῷ

εὖ καὶ ἐπισταμένως, καὶ ἐπὶ στάθμην ἴθυνα,

ἑρμῖν᾽ ἀσκήσας, τέτρηνα δὲ πάντα τερέτρῳ.

ἐκ δὲ τοῦ ἀρχόμενος λέχος ἔξεον, ὄφρ᾽ ἐτέλεσσα,

δαιδάλλων χρυσῷ τε καὶ ἀργύρῳ ἠδ᾽ ἐλέφαντι:

ἐκ δ᾽ ἐτάνυσσα ἱμάντα βοὸς φοίνικι φαεινόν. (23.190-201)

A densely -branched and narrow-leaved olive grew in the

courtyard,

Fully-grown and thriving: it was as thick as a pillar.

I built my bedroom walls around it, until I finished,

With well-joined stones, and I covered it with a roof well from

above,

And set in well-framed, close-fitting doors.

And then I cut off the olive tree's thick foliage,

I shaved off the outside of the trunk from the root with a bronze

tool

Well and skillfully, and straightened it with a plumbline,

Adorning the bedpost, I bored it all with an auger.

Beginning from this I carved my bed, until I finished,

Embellishing it with gold and silver and ivory:

I stretched out a bright red oxhide leather strap in it.

Every addition Odysseus makes to it is to make the bed into a more

valuable prestige item with his additions of elaborate carving, and inlays

of imported precious metals and ivory; even the suspension system for

the mattress, which would not be visible when the bed is in use, is

colored with an expensive imported dye which is named by its place of origin, Phoenicia (23.201). In a sense, the marriage bed is an embodiment of the marriage; the effort and prestige goods Odysseus puts into its production are his dedication to and value of his marriage. This part of the story is described precisely and consistently, which speaks to the narrative emphasis of Odysseus' choice to return to his marriage to Penelope.

Neither the reason Odysseus builds his marriage bed from a living, rooted olive tree nor his method of choosing the tree are explained. These ambiguities begin with the first word, θάμνος. It usually denotes a bush, shrub or thicket of trees, not the tall single tree with a dense canopy of branches overtop a thick trunk that the description of the bed's production implies and is typical of a healthy, mature olive tree. The description of how the olive tree is transformed into a bedpost implies that it has a thick, tall, and relatively straight trunk that only needed surface-depth carving to turn in into a completely straight and acceptably tall part of the elaborate marriage bed Odysseus builds. Only in this instance (*Od.* 23.190) is it definitely applied to a tree of this type.

This oddity becomes even more significant when the whole line is considered: "θάμνος ἔφυ τανύφυλλος ἐλαίης ἔρκεος ἐντός" (23.190) "A densely-branched and narrow-leaved olive grew in the courtyard". In order to form a coherent clause in English, my translation of this line glosses over some grammatical irregularities. θάμνος is taken to modify the other word for tree in the line, ἐλαίης (olive tree) and the verb of this clause, φύω, as taking this as its subject. However, θάμνος is the only noun in the nominative case here, ἐλαίης and its adjective τανύφυλλος (narrow-leaved) are both in the genitive. This cannot be resolved by making the subject be a partitive genitive construction, since in order for that to be grammatical both ἐλαίης and τανύφυλλος would need to be in the plural and the same plurality would make the sense of this clause not logically precede the rest of the description. It also cannot be reduced to θάμνος alone being the subject of φύω and ἐλαίης its object, which would change the sense of the clause to "a thicket produced a narrow-leaved olive tree", because φύω takes an accusative object. This grammatical ambiguity could be the result of condensing a longer passage that explicitly describes Odysseus' process of choosing a tree or could be meant to refer to a cult practice that need not be explained to the

Odyssey's contemporary audience; the facts that would disambiguate the line's reference are not extant.

    Odysseus' initial response to Penelope's test sheds light onto the rooted bedpost's meaning: "χαλεπὸν δέ κεν εἴη καὶ μάλ᾽ ἐπισταμένῳ, ὅτε μὴ θεὸς αὐτὸς ἐπελθὼν ῥηϊδίως ἐθέλων θείη ἄλλῃ ἐνὶ χώρῃ" (23.184-186), "hard would it be even for exceeding skill, unless a god personally comes near, willing to easily set it somewhere else". Sawing the rooted bedpost off of its roots should be a task equal to skill, so the difficulty must not be one presented by the physical bedpost, and the whole bed by extension, but one presented by the abstraction it embodies. The bed's nature is detailed again two lines later in the same speech by Odysseus, "ἀνδρῶν δ᾽ οὔ κέν τις ζωὸς βροτός, οὐδὲ μάλ᾽ ἡβῶν, ῥεῖα μετοχλίσσειεν, ἐπεὶ μέγα σῆμα τέτυκται", "no living mortal of men, even one of great youth, could easily move it, after it was made to be a great sign" (*Od.* 23.188). This additional line reinforces the divine status of the bed by repeating that it is resistant to mortal action, and begs a question at the same time. What was the bed made to be a sign of? The context of Odysseus' response to Penelope suggests that it was built to be a sign of Odysseus' identity, but the description of how the bed was built and the two mentions of godly power being necessary to move it says that it is a sign of Athena's support for Odysseus' marriage to Penelope.

The cult object this corresponds to is the sacred pillar, which represents the support of a deity for an important building in the late Bronze Age on the Syrio-Levantine coast. Pillar Worship, with various local twists, took place along the Eastern Mediterranean trade routes that flourished from about the tenth to eighth centuries BC: from the Syrio-Levantine coast through Cyprus to Crete, and from Crete to the Cyclades, mainland Greece and the West coast of Asia Minor (Ben-Shlomo: 2009, pg. 68). On the Syrio-Levantine coast, a deity is present in a stone pillar in the story of Jacob's ladder, "Jacob rose early in the morning, and he took the stone that he had put under his head and set it up for a pillar and poured oil on the top of it. He called that place Bethel" (Genesis 28.18-19). Jacob had slept with this rock under his head when he had the vision of the ladder and God stood beside him to tell Jacob of his support for Jacob's own and his descendants' future prosperity. Jacob declares that "Surely the Lord is in this place—and I did not know it! ... This is none other than the house of God, and this is the gate of heaven" (Genesis 28.16-17). Both this declaration and the name Jacob gives this place,

Bethel (בֵּית אֵל), mark it as an indwelling place of God (Arthur J. Evans:
1901, 112).

The theophany and promise of land on the way to arrange Jacob's
marriage in this story parallels the appearance of Athena under the olive
tree to aid in Odysseus' recovery of his marriage, land, and his son's
inheritance. At this point in the *Odyssey* (Od. 13. 370-375), Athena and
Odysseus plot against the suitors "ἱερῆς παρὰ πυθμέν᾽ ἐλαίης", "around
the bottom of a sacred olive tree". The olive tree in this passage that
Athena appears by in support of Odysseus can be interpreted as a parallel
to the olive tree that Odysseus fashioned into the rooted bedpost that
supports his position as Penelope's husband and king of Ithaca. This
parallel suggests that Athena may be considered to be present through a
sacred olive tree, even though she may not be visible.

Another source of evidence of pillar worship in the context of
cultural links between the Greek mainland and the Levantine coast that is
the story of Samson's life in Judges 14-16. It engages with cultural links
in two directions: from the fertile crescent in the East, and with Greece in
the West. His capture is by the only character in Samson's life named

other than himself and his father in the Bible, Delilah. Neither Samson's

mother, wife, nor any of the Philistines he interacts with are named, but

Delilah is, suggesting that she somehow has higher status than them.

Delilah strips Samson of his divinely sourced strength by shaving his hair

when he is made vulnerable with sex; this action parallels that of the

sacred prostitute Shamhat in *The Epic of Gilgamesh* (Tablet 1-2).

Shamhat takes the supernatural strength from Enkidu in order to bind him

to civilization and the purpose of his creation, namely to neutralize

Gilgamesh's destructive tendencies towards his people. Part of the

process of civilizing Enkidu, like the capture of Samson, is cutting his

hair; Shamhat undertakes civilizing Enkidu from a position of high status,

a position Delilah has as well.

Another piece of evidence of this trade corridor's function as a

corridor for religious and mythological stories is that Ishtar, the goddess

to whom Shamhat was a sacred prostitute, is a cognate of Aphrodite. The

Philistines are identified as being culturally tied to the Greeks in the Late

Bronze Age to early Iron Age (Killebrew: 2005, pg. 230). The two

goddesses share a story where they take a "dying god" lover: Ishtar's is

Tammuz (*Epic of Gilgamesh*, Tablet VI), Aphrodite's is Adonis (Saph

59). Adonis' name is derived from the Semitic Adonai, lord, which is likely the Semitic name of Tammuz, since no Semitic god referred to as Adonai participates in a story that follows a dying god's affair with a love goddess before he dies (W. Burkert: 1985 *Greek Religion*, 176–77). This suggests that the story from the inland Fertile Crescent was transmitted to the Greeks through the interpretation of a coastal Semitic people.

The worship in the form of a pillar was not specific to any particular god in the Bronze Age. It comes into the story of Samson's life at his death. Samson is brought out to be mocked at a sacrifice to Dagon, and is set between a pair of pillars, which he pulls down to kill all of the spectators and himself (Judges 16.23-31). It is impossible to build a house that is wholly supported by two pillars physically large enough in order for it to be possible that, "on the roof there were about three thousand men and women" (Judges 16.27). It follows that the pillars must be lending a supernatural support in order for their collapse to lead to the collapse of the entire building. Another thing to note in this passage is that although the sacrifice is to Dagon, the presence of a second pillar implies that another deity is also worshipped in the form of a pillar in this palace; the presence of both male and female worshippers suggests that

the other deity in the other pillar is a goddess.

The story of Samson and Delilah, along with its connections, is

sensible as the mythic representation of a ritual pattern of the sacrifice of

a male victim captured by a powerful woman to an urban god worshipped

in a pillar. This pattern is not developed yet in *The Epic of Gilgamesh*;

Shamhat does capture Enkidu on behalf of Ishtar so he may kill

Gilgamesh for Ishtar and this action does eventually result in Enkidu's

death, but his death for Ishtat was not what either Shamhat or Ishtar

intended. The story of Samson and Delilah takes this sequence of events

and applies it to the event of a sacrifice at a pillar cult: the prostitute

Delilah captures Samson for use in a sacrifice. This story, which was in a

position to be transmitted across the Aegean from the Syrio-Levantine

coast, is connected through the theme of a man's sacrifice for a goddess

to the story of Aphrodite and Adonis, which definitely traveled to Greece

from the Levantine coast, therefore, they could have travelled together as

a set of associated ideas.

A goddess definitely worshipped in conjunction with a tree is Ἑλένα Δενδρῖτις, Helen of the tree, whose cult was localized to the island of Rhodes. A description of this cult is found in Pausanias:

> ταύτην τὴν Πολυξώ φασιν ἐπιθυμοῦσαν Ἑλένην τιμωρήσασθαι τελευτῆς τῆς Τληπολέμου τότε, ὡς ἔλαβεν αὐτὴν ὑποχείριον, ἐπιπέμψαι οἱ λουμένῃ θεραπαίνας Ἐρινύσιν ἴσα ἐσκευασμένας· καὶ αὗται διαλαβοῦσαι δὴ τὴν Ἑλένην αἱ γυναῖκες ἀπάγχουσιν ἐπὶ δένδρου, καὶ ἐπὶ τούτῳ Ῥοδίοις Ἑλένης ἱερόν ἐστι Δενδρίτιδος. (Paus. 3.19.10)
>
> They say that this Polyxo desired to avenge the death of Tlepolemus on Helen, now that she had her in her power. So she sent against her when she was bathing handmaidens dressed up as Furies, who seized Helen and hanged her on a tree, and for this reason the Rhodians have a sanctuary of Helen of the Tree. (Jones & Ormerod 1918)

On the surface, the connection between this story and the worship of Helen of the tree may not be obvious. However, stories that attach a specific place to the death of a deity often serve to connect them to the location. An example from Pausanias is the tomb of Helen and Menelaus, "Μενελάου δέ ἐστιν ἐν αὐτῇ ναός, καὶ Μενέλαον καὶ Ἑλένην ἐνταῦθα ταφῆναι λέγουσιν" (3.19.9), "there is in the same place [Therapne] a temple of Menelaus, and they say Menelaus and Helen are buried there". This tomb is the physical link between Therapne and Menelaus, like the sacred tree is to Rhodesia and Helen; Helen's tree is an indwelling place for her presence.

The rooted olive bedpost implies that in the Bronze Age when contemporary customs were being absorbed into the Trojan Cycle, Athena took on a characteristic displayed by other deities, and was understood to appear near or manifest herself through her sacred tree, the olive tree. This suggests that such a tree, although never explicitly referred to as divine, may be a vessel and/or symbol of Athena in the contexts investigated above. It also shows that even though pillar worship in the Near East was not specifically associated with deities of a particular gender, in Greece pillar worship was linked to the worship of goddesses and not gods; the connection is to the Near Eastern stories that were imported with the concept of pillar worship, which included involved a mortal man serving and/or sacrificing himself for a goddess. The rooted bedpost of Odysseus and Penelope's marriage bed represents

Athena as a pillar of support for their marriage; Odysseus serves and endures toils for Athena. It partakes of her feminine gender.

2.3 The Arthurian Vulgate

The 13th-century *French Vulgate Cycle of Arthurian Romances* is rich in allegorical stories, which feature characters that are essentially inhuman and act in service of the message of their story. These stories engage with the practice of reading the world as a sign of divine meaning; the reader is to interpret the text like one would the Bible, looking for the hidden, abstract signified behind the concrete details of the story, which are the signifiers. The characters that represent a person's correct or incorrect action in the metaphor are male; the characters that represent abstract ideas are female; objects without a clear gender refer back to older texts. The *History of the Holy Grail* is a section of the larger prose cycle that is particularly heavy with metaphors that give messages to both the characters and the reader: the message of the rightness of holding true to God is expressed to both these audiences at once.

One story full of such characters and the message to keep true to God is the story of king Mordrain on the rock. In *The History of the Holy Grail*, king Mordrain's new faith after his conversion is tested on a barren island (Sommer I: 88-107). God transports him to a desolate rock, where both the Devil and Jesus come to him each day in disguise on a symbolically marked boat and each attempt to convince him to follow them. Even the island is full of symbolic meaning: it is referred to as a rock throughout Mordrain's stay, the story of its use by a pirate and the pirate's death by Pompey, and the bird that knocks Mordrain's bread into the sea are each meant to be read with their allegorical rather than literal meaning in mind to make sense of the episode. The episode is structured by binary oppositions between: God and the Devil, good and evil, darkness and light, the faithful and the faithless, human and supernatural, the Old and New Testaments, man and beast, heaven and earth, hot and cold, and male and female.

The place where Mordrain's faith is tested is defined as a barren island by what happens there: besides divine intervention, it is accessible by boat, and it has no arable land or human inhabitants. It has no name, it is "seulement la roce ou il estoit & cele roche estoit dedens la mer occeane" (Sommer I: 89), "only the rock where he was and this rock was within the ocean". This description of an island without calling it one points to a meaning beyond the denotative for la roce. As a symbol, the rock as appears in Jesus' naming of his disciple, "Et ego dico tibi, quia tu

es Petrus, et super hanc petram ædificabo Ecclesiam meam," (Matt.
16.18), "and I say to you that you are Peter, and on this rock I will build
my church", the name Peter literally means rock in the original Greek in
the same passage of the New Testament, "κἀγὼ δέ σοι λέγω ὅτι σὺ εἶ
πέτρος, καὶ ἐπὶ ταύτῃ τῇ πέτρᾳ οἰκοδομήσω μου τὴν ἐκκλησίαν", a
linguistic link which has been transmitted into the Vulgate version of the
Bible intact. This gives the rock a share of both genders: the masculine
πέτρος and the feminine la roce, marking it as an invitation to interpret
Mordrain's test on the rock in light of an intertext, namely the dialogue
between Jesus and Peter. It also sets a masculine interpreter to a feminine
text: Mordrain struggles to understand the rock and what it means to him.

The biblical dialogue takes place after the Pharisees and
Sadducees ask Jesus to point out a sign in the sky in the narrative of
Matthew. Jesus responds to them with a way of predicting if the weather
will be fair or stormy by whether the sky is red in the morning or the
evening, an answer which Jesus finishes speaking to the Pharisees and
Sadducees with a final comment, "Faciem ergo cæli dijudicare nostis:
signa autem temporum non potestis scire" (Matt. 16.4), "I would
therefore make to discern the sky for us: you cannot know the signs of

this time". He then proceeds to address his disciples, which is the

beginning of the dialogue that elicits the 'rock of my church' quote

above. The introduction of this dialogue through an intentional holding of

knowledge for Jesus' followers and keeping of the same away from non-

followers is reflected in Mordrain's story, he is told by the handsome

man to trust those that honor the cross like himself and not keep company

with those who do not (Sommer I: 94).

Even Jesus' description of himself through his powers to

Mordrain refers back to Matthew 16:

> il dist quil sauroit faire dun li biaus hom li lait homme & dune
>
> laide feme deuenir a si grant biaute comme nule biautes estre
>
> puet. & bien sacies nus autres ne le seit faire se iou ne li que
>
> apreng . & si sai faire dun poure homme riche & dun fol sage &
>
> dun has haut. (Sommer I: 93)
>
> He said he knew how to make, the beautiful man, an ugly man
>
> and an ugly woman into such a great beauty as no beauties can be.
>
> And you know well no others can do it if I do not teach them. And
>
> I know to make a poor man rich and a fool wise and a lowly man
>
> high.

This power to raise people from a lowly to a high state that the handsome man claims to have and be able to teach matches the power that Jesus gives Peter with the keys to the kingdom of heaven, "quodcumque ligaveris super terram, erit ligatum et in cælis: et quodcumque solveris super terram, erit solutum et in cælis." (Matt 16.19), "whatever you will bind on earth, will be bound and in heaven: and whatever you will loose on earth, will be loosed and in heaven". The passage in Matthew has the power of binding/loosing stand for control, which is typical of magico-religious texts in Antiquity.

Examples of this include: Ovid's description of the Lemuria as binding unquiet ghosts while leaving the head of household unbound (*Fasti 5.* 429-444), and *tabellae defixionis* that were bound to happen by literally folding, rolling up, and/or nailing the soft metal the curse is written on. The *defixiones*, which were widespread throughout Greco-Roman Antiquity, originating in the sixth century before the Common Era in Attica, continue to be produced in Britain until the fourth century of the Common Era[21] (Adams: 1992, 24); the actual text of the curse

---

[21] A late example from *Aquae Sulis* reads: Seu gen(tili)s seu C/h(r)istianus qu<i=AE>cumque utrum vir / [u]trum mulier utrum puer utrum puella / utrum s[er]vus utrum liber mihi Annia[n]/o

seldom uses the language of binding. With the widespread adoption of Christianity, binding/loosing as the ideal of control was replaced by the omnipotence of God expressed through language as the ideal of control. A story that shows the transition from the control as binding model to control as effective language is the story of the liberation of St. Peter. King Herod has Peter imprisoned in anticipation of having him publicly executed, and he waited in prison:

> Oratio autem fiebant sine intermissione ab ecclesia ad Deum pro eo. Cum autem producturus eum esset Herodes, in ipsa nocte erat Petrus dormiens inter duos milites, vinctus catenis duabus: et custodes ante ostium custodiebant carcerem. Et ecce angelus Domini astitit, et lumen refulsit in habitaculo: percussoque latere Petri, excitavit eum, dicens: Surge velociter. Et ceciderunt catenæ de manibus ejus. (Acts 12.5-7)

---

ma{n}tut<i=E>ne de bursa mea s(e)x argente[o]s / furaverit(!) tu
d[o]mina dea ab ipso perexi[g]/e [3 eo]s si mihi per [f]raudem aliquam
inde p/r(a)eg[u]stum(?) dederit nec sic(!) ipsi dona sed ut sangu/inem
suum (r)eputes qui mihi hoc i<r=N>rogaverit (EDCS -08600464)
Whether gentile or Christian, whoever, either man or woman, either boy
or girl, either slave or free, from me Annianus, in the morning stole from
my purse six silver coins, you lady goddess from him will extract if from
me by a lie from Praegustum, he will give not this gift but so that you
judge his blood which is asked for by me.

But prayer was made without ceasing of the church unto God for

him. And when Herod would have brought him forth, the same

night Peter was sleeping between two soldiers, bound with two

chains: and the keepers before the door kept the prison. And,

behold, the angel of the Lord came upon him, and a light shined

in the prison: and he smote Peter on the side, and raised him up,

saying, Arise up quickly. And his chains fell off from his hands.

God, through the angel, exercises a superior form of power in this story:

one that is abstract, verbal, and unlimited by the nature of the concrete,

embodied power of the bonds. The name Jesus in disguise gives, "tout en

tout" (Sommer I: 93), "All in All", fits the espousal of this sort of all-

encompassing power of language not restricted to the physical or

metaphorical act of binding in the *Arthurian Vulgate*. What also changes

is the way power is gendered: the binding model of control is not

attached to a particular gender, the one who would and can bind has the

power over the bound, but the linguistic power has chosen a gendered

system: the feminine church (ecclesia) asks the masculine God to act

through his male angels to free Peter. Direct control is masculine; indirect

control is feminine.

The passage in the *History of the Holy Grail* picks up on the binary opposition between high heaven and low earth, not the binding, in the passage in Matthew. The rest of Mordrain's first encounter with Jesus in disguise as the handsome man also follows the template of Jesus' dialogue with his disciples in Matthew 16. The purpose of Jesus' appearance and dialogue with his follower(s) in both places are also related. Peter earns his name from Jesus by correctly naming who Jesus is to his followers:

> Dicit illis Jesus: Vos autem, quem me esse dicitis? Respondens Simon Petrus dixit: Tu es Christus, Filius Dei vivi. Respondens autem Jesus, dixit ei: Beatus es Simon Bar Jona: quia caro et sanguis non revelavit tibi, sed Pater meus, qui in cælis est. (Matt. 16.15-17)
>
> He saith unto them, but whom say ye that I am? And Simon Peter answered and said, Thou art the Christ, the Son of the living God. And Jesus answered and said unto him, Blessed art thou, Simon Bar-jona: for flesh and blood hath not revealed it unto thee, but my Father which is in heaven.

Mordrain, in contrast to Peter, asks for Jesus' name. He is ignorant of Jesus' father, and needs to find an answer on the rock before he can pass his test and leave with Jesus. Before he vanishes at the end of his first

visit, Jesus warns Mordrain against those who do not honor the cross,

which is the symbol of Christian faith, like he warns his disciples against

the teachings of the Pharisees and Sadducees before the Peter the rock

quote (Matt 16.6-12). The warning is also relevant because it presents a

correspondence between two binary sets that will appear in Mordrain's

story: that between masculinity and heaven and between femininity and

earth. Jesus and the Devil are male and female respectively, following

this correspondence.

Another element of the stories surrounding this quote that is

reworked into Mordrain's test on the rock is the use of bread as a symbol.

The morning after Mordrain resists the Devil the second time, he finds a

loaf of bread from God. Bread is mentioned in the relevant area of

Matthew through Jesus' warning against the yeast of the Pharisees and

the Sadducees when they had gathered without having remembered to

bring bread (Matt 16.5). Jesus warns his disciples to avoid the yeast of

their bread, but since this warning confuses the disciples, he points them

in the right direction:

Quare non intelligitis, quia non de pane dixi vobis: Cavete a

fermento pharisæorum et sadducæorum? Tunc intellexerunt quia

non dixerit cavendum a fermento panum, sed a doctrina

pharisæorum et sadducæorum (Matt 16.11-12)

How is it that ye do not understand that I spake it not to you

concerning bread, that ye should beware of the leaven of the

Pharisees and of the Sadducees? Then understood they how that

he bade them not beware of the leaven of bread, but of the

doctrine of the Pharisees and of the Sadducees.

By analogy with this story attached to the story that elicits the rock of the

church quote, which is referred to in the name of the island, the loaf of

bread in Mordrain's story is also not meant to be interpreted literally.

However, it takes its meaning from another story of the New Testament

that the story of king Mordrain on the rock refers to in another way. This

story also sets a contrast between the evil teachings (doctrina, f) and their

non-evil symbol, yeast (fermento, n).

The bread can also be read against a part of the Old Testament,

the gift of manna from heaven, or a part of the New Testament, the story

of the temptation of Christ. The temptation of Christ is recounted in differing specifics and levels of detail in all three synoptic Gospels. The versions that use bread as a symbol are those of Matthew and Luke, both mention bread with almost the same exchange between the Devil and Jesus. In Matthew 4.3-4:

> Et accedens tentator dixit ei: Si Filius Dei es, dic ut lapides isti panes fiant. Qui respondens dixit: Scriptum est: Non in solo pane vivit homo, sed in omni verbo, quod procedit de ore Dei.
>
> And when the tempter came to him, he said, If thou be the Son of God, command that these stones be made bread. But he answered and said, it is written, Man shall not live by bread alone, but by every word that proceedeth out of the mouth of God.

And almost the same in Luke 4.3-4:

> Dixit autem illi diabolus: Si Filius Dei es, dic lapidi huic ut panis fiat. Et respondit ad illum Jesus: Scriptum est: Quia non in solo pane vivit homo, sed in omni verbo Dei.
>
> And the devil said unto him, If thou be the Son of God, command this stone that it be made bread. And Jesus answered him, saying, It is written, That man shall not live by bread alone, but by every word of God.

This exchange between Jesus and the Devil sheds some light on the reason for including the loaf of bread that the bird wasted before Mordrain can eat it. The bread simply appears while Mordrain slept; he awoke hungry, "Et quant il se fu longement plains de sa mesaise si uit sor. j . des degres de la roce" (Sommer I: 102), "and when he was himself far away he saw the bread of his ill-ease on one of the stairs of the rock". Mordrain goes to eat the bread, but is stopped from eating it by the bird.

By wasting the bread and punishing Mordrain for attempting to eat it, unaware of its meaning, the bird ironically acts in his interest, much like the Devil does when he sets Jesus up to reject him and grow spiritually by tempting him in the desert. Both the bread and the rock, which are not spoken of in clearly gendered terms[22], point to an interpretation using an intertext as the symbol key. The intertext that the bird took the meaning of the bread from is the story of manna from heaven in the Old Testament (Exodus 16). Seeing that Mordrain was about to avail himself of God's help in the desert, the strange bird stops

---

[22] Other than their grammatical genders: feminine for the rock and masculine for the bread. The text does tend to add determiners that reveal the gender of rock (la, cele…) more than the bread, which is left without a le or cel, but in the few instances referring to the bread present in the story, this is not conclusive.

him in order to help the Devil separate him from God, unaware of its

incorrect reading of the sign.

The bird that wastes Mordrain's bread is one of a type that the

narrative segues into a detailed description of as soon as it appears. Its

life cycle is as follows: its clutch of three eggs are so cold by nature that

they need to be warmed up by a special stone from the valley of Ebron in

order to hatch, named at the end of the story as piratite. The mother bird

must rub the stone to release its heat, but to do so reduces her to ash by

the time her eggs hatch; the hatchlings are nourished by her ashes. Two

of them are male, and they fight to the death over the one female, named

Serpens Lyons right before the stone is in the narrative (Sommer I: 102-

103). This story is striking both in what it includes and what it omits.

It goes into great detail as to how this type of bird reproduces,

including going to an aspect of humoural theory for recourse to formulate

the explanation. The aspect invoked is the hot/cold binary used in

humoural theory. The bird's eggs are cold, so much so that they need to

be exposed to extreme heat that cannot be provided by the mother bird's

body heat and is in fact lethal to her in order to hatch. This detail suggests two things: that the mother bird is also cold, and that self-sacrifice is important to the bird's meaning to Mordrain's story, in which it is embedded. Humoural theory involves a set of correspondences between the classical elements, a set of binaries that includes temperature and elements, and a set of four bodily fluids called humours (Singer, 2016). Cold is the feminine temperature, and hot is the masculine one; the story this bird is embedded within has set up the correspondence between masculinity and Jesus and between femininity and the Devil with their respective disguised forms.

The name given to the female bird born, Serpens Lyons, adds to the meaning of her mother's sacrifice. It is a combination of two different common nouns for types of animal, a snake and a lion, the characteristics of which her species displays. The first animal, the serpent, names the bird as an agent against God like the serpent that tempts Eve in the Garden of Eden. In the traditions of Bible exegesis available in Latin in the twelfth and thirteenth centuries, especially those that call their support from the later Books of the Bible, the serpent in the story of the fall is identified with the Satan that appears in the Book of Job, the Devil that appears in the temptation of Christ (Matt 4.1-11, Mark 1.12-13, Luke 4.1-13) and the Devil as a serpent in the Book of Revelation (12.9, 20.2).

The other animal in Serpens Lyons' name, the lion, is connected to the other aspect of the bird's life cycle: the mother's noble sacrifice of herself for her young's survival. Within the sources of the *History of the Holy Grail*, the story of Iwein and his lion from the 12th century sheds light on its symbolism. In the *Yvain, the Knight of the Lion* of Chrétien de Troyes, Iwein acquires the companionship of a lion on his search for a balance between his knightly and husbandly responsibilities by saving it from a serpent's attack. With the lion's help, Yvain fights for a series of women before reconciling with his wife Laudine: he defeats the giant who would have kidnapped and sexually abused Gawain's niece, the two sons of a devil and a mortal woman who had been extorting a tribute of damsels to produce fine cloth for them, champions a coheiress disinherited by her older sister, and saves Luncte from burning as a traitor for advising Laudine to marry Yvain as a favor to Yvain.

The fiery serpent and the lion are both masculine and antagonistic towards each other directly, belonging completelty to the masculine sphere of combat, and contrast with the ladies, who participate in combat indirectly through their knights and directly work with textiles and support knights finincially. The work as a whole reinforces the reciprocal rights and responsibilities of a knight and lady. The two genders are kept in separate individuals that interact through set social roles, one gender per character; the strange bird of Mordrain's rock does not respect this distinction. The bird mixes the natures of serpent, lion, and bird into one animal, the noble and predatory symbolic meanings of the lion, the active lioness of the Old Testament and passive self-sacrifice of the New Testament, and a male individual and a masculine attack with a feminine humoural makeup; it is a monstrous category confusion.

The narrative of the *Arthurian Vulgate* does not include which of the birds attacks Mordrain and wastes his bread or any explicit mention of the father of Serpens Lyons and her brothers. It could be one of several of them: Serpens Lyons, her surviving brother, or possibly their father. The beginning and end of the extended description of the bird through its life cycle, which connect to the main story of Mordrain's stay on the rock, do not explicitly state which of the birds mentioned or implied to exist is the embedded story: namely, the introduction of the bird: "& il esgarde si uoit vn oisel descendre uers lui tant grant & tant diuers que

onques mais tel oisel nauoit ueu" (Sommer I: 102), "and he moved his

attention such and saw a bird descend towards him the biggest and most

multicolored that ever was but such a bird he had not seen", and the

return to the main story "Itels estoit li oisiaus dont ie vous parole qui

descendi sor le roi" (Sommer I: 103), "the same was the bird which I told

you had descended on the king", contain no clues as to which of the birds

in the story of their species. The word oisel is grammatically masculine,

which is the standard for animals of unknown or unspecified gender;

what defines the bird as the only male one mentioned and still alive in the

inserted story, Serpens Lyons' brother, is his violence against Mordrain.

Serpens Lyons' surviving brother is the only one of the birds to have won

anything through prowess in battle, namely mastery of the only named

bird herself.

The story of the bird's reproduction is suggestive of what it

symbolizes in another way. Throughout it, the story sets up a trinity of

birds that apes the one of God the Father, Son, and Holy Spirit. The

doctrine of the trinity is laid out in two places in the *Arthurian Vulgate*:

in Joseph's explanation of the vision of Evalach (Sommer I: 27-28) and in the prologue of *The History of the Holy Grail* (Sommer I: 3-7). In

Josephus' explanation of the vision of king Evalach, the trinity appears as

an infinitely tall tree with three equal trunks: the first one to appear is

God the Father, the second one that appears out of the first is God the

Son, and the third that branches out of the union between the first two is

the Holy Spirit.

In the prologue of *The History of the Holy Grail*, the narrative

begins with the author greeting and blessing the reader for believing in

the Holy Trinity introduction, directly addressing the book to "Chil ki se

tient & aii iuge plus petit & au plus peceor de monde. Mande salus au

commenchement de ceste estoire [h 2] A tos cheaus ki lor cuers ont & lor

creance en la sainte trinite" (Sommer I: 3), "to he who holds himself and

was judged the most small and the biggest sinner in the world. I send a

blessing at the beginning of this history to all those who have their hearts

and their belief in the Holy Trinity". Jesus then appears to the

deliberately anonymus author to assuage his doubts about the Trinity; the

author is brought up by an angel as a disembodied spirit to see himself

"la force de la trinite [h 20] apertement . Car iou i vi deuiseement Ie pere

& Ie fil & Ie saint esperit. Et si vi que ces . iij . persones repairoient a vne deite & a vne poissance" (Sommer I: 7), "the force of the Trinity

apparent. For I saw distinctly the Father and the Son and the Holy Spirit.

And so I saw that these three persons rejoined as one deity and one

power".

This prologue is addressed directly to its readers to make them

more confident in their faith: offering the use of the text to one who

believes in the Trinity and then bolstering that belief with proof. The

bird's purpose is to demonstrate what the Holy Trinity is not: it is not a

monstrous category confusion, the perverted version, of which "li diables

aime le seruice" (Sommer I: 102), "the Devil loves the service" is. The

bird, like the Trinity, is three in one, but serves the Devil rather than rules

as God. It is also called the opposite gender as the Trinity, the bird is le

oisel, the Trinity la trinite, signalling the bird's opposition to the Trinity.

Like the other symbols without a clear gender, the meaning of the strange

bird, that is an unnamed male and a named female sprung from a dead

female, is in its intertexts.

The main contrast of the episode is between Mordrain and

Pompey's stories; Mordrain's experience on the rock strengthens his

Christian faith, Pompey rejects conversion. Pompey goes to the rock to eradicate Forcair and his band; he besieges the pirates in their fortress carved into the high ground of the rock, and wins after lighting two fires at the base and fighting two skirmishes, finding the pirates above dead after the second fire is put out. Forcair himself is captured by Pompey after the second skirmish but before the second fire is lit, and tossed in the sea with the bodies of the other pirates to drown. Pompey leaves the island and stables his horses in the Temple of Jerusalem; Pompey is rebuked by the father of Simeon for this act and is afterward defeated in everything he undertakes (Sommer I: 92).

On the rock, Mordrain faces the Devil and Jesus in disguise twice each. Jesus appears as a handsome man and arrives on a boat that has a white sail with a red cross on it; The Devil appears as a beautiful woman and arrives on a black-draped and black-sailed ship followed by a tempest. The visits from Jesus in disguise correspond to the lightings of a fire by Pompey's men; the visits from the Devil in disguise correspond to Pompey's skirmishes with the pirates. Each visit from Jesus strengthens Mordrain's faith, kindling a fire in him against the darkness that terrifies him after the Devil's first visit, "Et quant il ot longement este en ces tenebres si perdi si le sens & le memoire que de cose quil eust veue ne li

souenoit" (Sommer I: 96-97), "and when he had for such a long time

been in these shadows that he lost his sense and memory so much that

because of it what he had seen he did not remember". This instance of

Mordrain passing out corresponds to Pompey passing out due to his

injuries in his first skirmish with the pirates (Sommer I: 91).

Mordrain's second encounter with the Devil corresponds to

Pompey's second skirmish with the pirate band; Pompey's capture of

Forcair corresponds to Mordrain's defeat of the Devil in a verbal contest.

The contrast between Pompey and Mordrain is in their relationship to the

Church. Mordrain is a convert to Christianity through Josephus, and

Pompey rejects conversion. The contrast between Pompey and Mordrain

forms a metanarrative with a message for the reader, the message being

that a leader without the favor of God will fail. The two men contrast the

correct and incorrect attitudes for a man in a position of secular

leadership towards God. Pompey and Mordrain, as is fitting to the

message of the story, correspond to each other in all aspects other than

their relationship with God: they are both human men, both are

overwhelmed in their earthly body but prevail due to a heavenly quality of their mission (Mordrain holds to God and Pompey does justice against the pirates).

In an episode that parallels Josephus' correct interpretation of Evalach's vision on the first night Josephus and his followers spend in his palace at Sarras (Sommer I: 27-28), Josephus interprets the dream Duke Ganor has the first night Josephus and his followers spend in his castle (Sommer I 219-220). The vision of Evalach includes an image of people in one of the trees of the Trinity, some of whom bathe in its sap and do well while those that do not suffer. This is a metaphor for the effect of the choice to accept baptism, or being cleansed with the blood of the lamb, and convert on a person, male or female.

The dream of Duke Ganor uses a different metaphorical image to convince him to convert himself and his people; it has the duke see a clear stream with white people in it and a black cloud over black people, who are trapped in a valley while the white ones move freely. When "tous ces clers & tous ces maistres deuant lui" (Sommer I 219), "all his clerks and all his masters before him" do not know what the dream means, he calls for the Christians to explain it. Josephus speaks for the group and says that the stream is the water of baptism, the white people

are the members of his group, who had accepted baptism, and the black

people are those among the group who had fallen into sin, the valley was

"del ual de plours & de larmes" (Sommer I 220), "the valley of laments

and of tears" that trapped sinners.

Where in the first episode, the message is intended for Evalach, to

convince him to convert himself and his people, and for the readers, to

convince them that their religion is the right one. The second message is

for Josephus' followers, warning them that if they did not continue to

cleanse themselves they would become black with sin and fall into the

valley and for the readers, warning them of the same. The metaphor of

Duke Ganor's dream is less appropriate to the context of the story and

more appropriate to the text's message to the readers than that of

Evalach's vision. Duke Ganor's dream only makes sense as a message to

him telling him to become a Christian with his followers by analogy with

its doublet, Evalach's vision.

These doublets use both male and female metaphorical figures to

say that both the men and women under the male leader's power should become Christians with their leader and cleanse themselves of sin.

Women and men are equal as followers of God or of secular leaders, but

men are leaders, women are not. The stories of Mordrain and Pompey on

the rock also equate masculinity with leadership: Pompey and Mordrain

are leaders, as God leads the Devil before they separate. This

correspondence between masculinity and leadership and femininity and

subordination fits with the double standard of piety shown to the three

couples near the beginning of the *History of the Holy Grail*; the men:

Joseph, Mordrain, and Nacien, owe their service only to God, the wives:

Joseph's unnamed wife, Sarrasinte, and Flegentine, owe the same to both

God and their husbands. A faithful man has one lord, God; a faithful

woman has both God and her husband as her lord.

3 Textuality

The *Odyssey* and the *Arthurian Vulgate*'s different embedded views of textuality stem from their different methods of composition and contemporary discourses on composition. As the product of oral composition, the *Odyssey*'s notions of textuality are embedded in a context where performance and continuous feedback from the work's audience is assumed. The *Arthurian Vulgate*'s textuality is thoroughly literate by its frequent mentions of written sources, how the material came to be written in the first place, and other metanarrative elements. Beyond this essential difference between text in an oral and a literate culture, each culture brings gender into how they talk about the process of composition. The *Odyssey* genders composition in two ways depending on which image of composition it uses: the image of composing a story for a specific person, or for a performance to a broad audience, each for a purpose; the use both types of composition is shown to be an assertion of power. The *Arthurian Vulgate* genders composition in its oral and written forms by directly and indirectly commenting on the process of composing within the narrative, using metanarrative elements, and reiterations of the same story. Both use characters as signs to make statements about composition.

3.1 The *Odyssey*

Rhetoric is a source of power in the *Odyssey*; both Penelope and Odysseus accomplish their heroic feats with the aid of convincing speech. Odysseus' rival, Circe has speech as her divine power; she is referred to as "Κίρκη ἐυπλόκαμος, δεινὴ θεὸς αὐδήεσσα" (*Od* 12.150), "fair-tressed Circe, dread god of human speech" by Odysseus when he formally names her as the giver of a favorable wind for him to leave Aeaea after Elpenor's funeral. She is also named with the same line by this ability before Odysseus and his men carry out her instructions to raise the shade of Tiresias (11.1), and when they arrive on Aeaea for the first time (10.136). These contexts reflect when Odysseus and crew fall under Circe's sphere of influence: when they enter it when they find Aeaea for the first time and leave for the final time, and use Circe's knowledge move towards obtaining their goal.

Circe also possesses the Sirens' ability to lure men to a dead end with song. Odysseus' men are drawn to her past her tame transformed men as beasts by her singing, "Κίρκης δ' ἔνδον ἄκουον ἀειδούσης ὀπὶ καλῇ, / ἱστὸν ἐποιχομένης μέγαν ἄμβροτον, οἷα θεάων / λεπτά τε καὶ χαρίεντα καὶ ἀγλαὰ ἔργα πέλονται" (10.221-223), "I heard Circe singing within with a beautiful voice, / approaching the upright, large, immortal work, of the sort of goddesses / and made it refined and charming and bright". Circe's doublet, Calypso, is also recognized as a goddess of speech when Odysseus recounts that he "νῆσον ἐς Ὠγυγίην πέλασαν θεοί, ἔνθα Καλυψὼ / ναίει ἐυπλόκαμος, δεινὴ θεὸς αὐδήεσσα" (12.448-449), "approached the island Ogygia, of the god, there Calypso / fair-tressed indeed, dread god of human speech dwells". These two goddesses are both able to oblige Odysseus to stay on their respective island with their power of speech; it takes Athena's intervention through Zeus and Hermes to free Odysseus each time, since Odysseus' mortal speech does not equal divine speech.

In the hall of the king Alcinous, Odysseus convinces Alcinous to send him home with gifts by convincing him that he is the type of man Alcinous can profit from a reciprocal gift-giving relationship. Odysseus accomplishes this by his narration of his exploits since he left Troy. He sets up two episodes that contrast Odysseus and his man Polites' reactions to the peril of attractive song. The story of Odysseus and crew's encounter with the Sirens and the leader of the advance party and his men's first encounter with Circe form an inverted parallel with each other. In each, there is a contrast between how one man and everyone else experiences the peril of attractive song. Odysseus allows himself to listen to the Sirens without danger by having himself restrained by his men, who are kept safe by their inability to hear the Sirens and row the boat past them (12.165-200). Polites follows Circe's song into her cave along with the others, straight into her power without any precautions. It is Eurylochus, who is not the leader of the party, who hangs back and is able to return to tell Odysseus of Circe's transformative powers (10.208-260).

Speech is also an attribute of Leukothea's human self, Ino, from before she became a goddess. This is described as: "τὸν δὲ ἴδεν Κάδμου θυγάτηρ, καλλίσφυρος Ἰνώ, / Λευκοθέη, ἣ πρὶν μὲν ἔην βροτὸς αὐδήεσσα, / νῦν δ᾽ ἁλὸς ἐν πελάγεσσι θεῶν ἐξ ἔμμορε τιμῆς." (5.333-335), "I saw the following, the daughter of Cadmus, beautifu-ankled Ino, / Leukothea, who before was of a mortal voice, / now is god of the salt in the sea as her portion of honor". This name for honor, τιμή, is used of gifts given as the physical form of prestige, including female slaves. Ino receives this power over the valuable salt of the sea in exchange for doing something. Τιμή is typically used of the compensation a warrior receives for his participation in a raid; what Leukotheia had done to deserve such

a reward is not mentioned in the *Odyssey* and is contradictory elsewhere

(Graves 1955)[23].

Demodocus and the Sirens both sing of their subject's κλέος:

Demodocus sings as a bard to spread the renown of his subjects

throughout the halls of the warrior and landowning elite, one such

performance his subject happens to attend on his way back to society and

the rewards of his heroics; the Sirens monstrously reverse this process by

feeding tales of his own κλέος back to the subject and the others in the

audience and luring them to a dead end on their uninhabited island,

whence the subject's fame cannot spread. Both Demodocus and the

Sirens sing of Odysseus' fame to him in their respective ways. In

Alcinous' hall full of kings, Odysseus gives away his identity with tears

that only king Alcinous sees at Demodocus' telling of the exploits of

heroes of Troy generally (8.43-96), and specifically Odysseus' in the

story of the Trojan Horse (8.471-525), and thereby furthers his cause to

---

[23] She was either: the mortal Ino transformed into a goddess by the Olympian Gods out of pity for her death jumping off a cliff into the sea due to Hera's infliction of madness upon her for sheltering Dionysus or the nymph Halia (of the sea) who married Posidaon.

get home by giving king Alcinous a true sign of his identity. On the trip

past the Sirens' island, Odysseus alone hears the Sirens sing of his glory

(12.165-200), which is not the ideal result of hearing his κλέος

disseminated to a crowd of Odysseus' social equals who would think

better of him.

The two are contrasted in more ways than this. Each of their

actions performing a song about Odysseus is described with a different

verb: ἀείδειν for Demodocus, βοᾶν for the Sirens. Ἀείδειν is the typical

word to describe the performance of epic; it covers both the sound of the

song and the lyre accompanying it. Βοᾶν is the typical word for shouting

or calling; it is not typically used to describe the performance of a song,

but the issue of loud, inhuman sounds, like the wind and waves, and of

disorganized, emotional yelling. The Sirens song is quoted, but

Demodocus' songs about Troy are summarized. This primes the

Odyssey's listener to think of Demodocus as impossibly skilled, taking

this impression from Odysseus' reaction and the respect the Phaeacians

have for him, and pick apart the Sirens' song, which had the same level

of detail and attention to style as the summary of Demodocus' song. The

praise in song from Demodocus is presented as valuable to Odysseus, the same from the Sirens is presented as not only an inherently worse song, but also as useless for the spread of his fame. Odysseus' encounter with the Sirens is a feat in itself, not a method of praising and disseminating a heroic feat.

In Odysseus' hall on Ithaca, Penelope convinces the suitors to give her wooing gifts (18.250-280). She introduces her availability due to her husband's wish she should remarry if he did not return before Telemachus became a man, which the suitors believe is true despite how Penelope tricked them into believing that she would marry one of them after she had finished weaving a shroud for Laertes, then weaving by day and unweaving by night (2.88-110). She induces the suitors to offer her gifts with a request covered in a complaint: Penelope complains that a woman of her wealth ought to receive competitive gifts from her suitors, who should not take advantage of her household's hospitality. Odysseus watches and is happy that Penelope has been able to draw wealth from the suitors while "νόος δέ οἱ ἄλλα μενοίνα" (18.283), "her mind was on other things" she was not sincerely interested in marrying one of the suitors.

The difference between these masculine, on the part of Odysseus and Demodocus, and feminine, on the part of the Sirens, Circe, and Calypso, uses of formal speech is their direction. The masculine version is directed outward; the feminine is directed inward. Both Odysseus and Demodocus seek to form new reciprocal relationships beyond their household with their speech, the Sirens, Circe, and Calypso all unilaterally seek to capture the target of their speech and keep him in their household; Penelope seeks to take advantage of a preexisting relationship. The same outward, social, and masculine speech is also used by Zeus when he is asked to intervene for Odysseus' wellbeing by Athena and Hermes when he acts on Zeus' behalf. Calypso responds to Hermes in kind when she protests the double standard of acceptance for affairs between gods and goddesses and mortals (5.118-128)

Odysseus is the hero of masculine speech in the *Odyssey*; Penelope is the heroine of feminine speech. Odysseus' uses of speech exemplify the masculine traits shown throughout the epic: he constantly attempts to form more guest-friendships in his effort to return home. Penelope's exemplifies feminine traits: she speaks to passively elicit offers of what she wants, which is to maintain her position as the wealthy wife of Odysseus, rather than actively ask for the same or seek to form a

new social bond with any of the suitors by marrying one. The two of

them each keep to the characteristic speech of their gender, but the divine

characters Zeus and Circe all use the other gender's style of speech: Zeus

by indirectly helping Odysseus through Hermes and Circe by directly

criticizing a prevailing social attitude.

3.2 The Arthurian Vulgate

The competition between theology and rhetoric is a tension expressed through many of the stories worked into the *Arthurian Vulgate*. The *Arthurian Vulgate*'s authors belonged to the literate class of people in the twelfth and thirteenth centuries; most of whom were either monastics or educated by the same. Text is treated as an exercise in theology when the *Arthurian Vulgate* pairs a section of metaphorical text, a signifier, with an interpretation to explain it, a signified. This adheres, to varying degrees of closeness, to Augustine's opinions on reading the Bible and the world for divine meaning that he puts forward in his writing (*The Confessions of St Augustine* 8.12). The use of these interpreted messages to convince either a character or the reader is an exercise in rhetoric. The various stories that have a prophetic dream be described, then correctly interpreted by a spiritually empowered character and those that have the same type of interpretor prove the virtue of a woman follow this model the most. Merlin and several of the holy men accompanying the Grail from the Holy Land in *The History of the Holy Grail* are the interpreters in this type of story. The interpreter is masculine, and the text feminine.

In the *Arthurian Vulgate*, Merlin is distinguished by his rhetorical

prowess. His abilities are explained by his origin as the child of a demon

and a human woman; the demons, seeking to create the Antichrist, have

the one of them who is capable impregnate a woman. His preternatural

intelligence and knowledge Merlin inherited from his father, and his soul

and free will he inherited from his mother. Merlin's first exploits in the

History of Merlin are rhetorical ones: he defends his mother from being

burned at the stake for having sex with a demon (Sommer II: 3-19).

Merlin acts as the ideal rhetorician, reading the text of his mother and her

judge's mother's virtue accurately with his supernatural insight and using

this knowledge to defend his mother. This version of Merlin's

conception, birth, and early prowess is geared towards proving that

Merlin, a rhetorician, is and can be on the side of God. It is therefore a

text of rhetoric made on behalf of Merlin, and those with rhetorical skills,

to persuade the reader that Merlin, and rhetoricians, is and can be on the

side of God.

This is made apparent by a comparison of this version in the *Book*

of Merlin (Sommer II: 3-19) that is biased towards Merlin and

rhetoricians, with the one in the *Book of Lancelot* (Sommer III: 20-21), which is biased against Merlin and rhetoricians. The version in the *Book of Lancelot* presents Merlin's conception as the result of female moral failure allowing a demon to reproduce with a human. This connection to sin biases the story against Merlin by presenting him as the result of a monstrous conversion: a woman turned away from God and her husband and towards the Devil and adultery instead of the other way around. Although many other stories of the origin of a hero credit his conception to the sin of sex outside the bond of marriage, these stories do not have the damsel choose to have sex and a child with a demon outside of marriage instead of getting married to an appropriate man like this story does.

Another of the Latin Church Fathers whose opinions are relevant to how rhetoric is connected to gender is Ambrosuis. He is the source of the doctrine about the Virgin Mary that is described in detail in the *History of the Holy Grail*. Ambrosius argued that the Virgin Mary remained a virgin after Jesus' birth, following the line of logic that: the mind and the body were separate, Mary possessed virtue of both mind and body (of which virginity is a virtue of both), celestial and earthly things did not effect each other, Jesus is spiritual (celestial), and wisdom (a mental/celestial virtue) is constant where folly is inconsistent (CSEL

LXIV: 122-123). At the end of this train of thought is the conclusion that

the Virgin Mary remained a virgin despite having given birth to Jesus

since the effect of birth on her body could not effect her constant spiritual

virtue of virginity, although it is not explicitly stated. This doctrine is

spelled out explicitly and explained twice in *The History of the Holy*

Grail through two different metaphors, which are interpreted in the

narrative: the metaphor of the child's entrance, and the metaphor of the

lily and the rosebush.

The first metaphor is not explained by Josephus, but Ambrosius'

position on the Virgin Mary to king Evalach is told with the metaphor of

the child's entrance, which is literally shown and explained to Evalach in

a vision (Sommer I: 28-29). This message is from God to king Evalach.

The child enters and exits his room without using the door, and a

supernatural voice explains the child as: "ensi comme li enfes est entres

& issus en ta cambre. ensi entra li fiex dieu en la uirgene marie sans mal

metre sa uirginite" (Sommer I: 29), "as how the child entered and exited

from your room, so entered the son of God into the Virgin Mary without

doing ill to her virginity". This explanation is directed at Evalach in response to Josephus' failure to convince Evalach of the Virgin Mary's nature with rhetoric. The figures are naturalistically gendered according to what they represent: the child (li enfes) is masculine like Jesus and the room (ta cambre) is feminine like the Virgin Mary.

The metaphor of the lily and the rosebush for the Virgin Mary's nature is introduced to the narrative by duke Ganor, who challenges his philosophers to refute Celidoine's explanation of it that is not included in the narrative directly (Sommer I: 220-222. Duke Ganor summarizes the position Celidoine had explained earlier in his challenge, which is: "signour vous deues parlera celydo[i]ne [que] dicele dame con apele uirge marie meire ihesu crist ne puet nus hons naistre en tel maniere quele fust pucele auant & apres" (Sommer I: 220), "your lord obliges you to tell Celidoine who said that the lady one calls the Virgin Mary mother of Jesus Christ could not birth a nude man in such a manner that she was a virgin before and after". Lucan refutes this position with an appeal to the way the world naturally works for human women, to which Josephus responds with a prayer to "chele glorieuse dame sour qui tu veus tel menchoinge esprouer" (Sommer I: 220), "this glorious lady of whom you want to prove such a lie" to stop Lucan. In response, Lucan is made to gouge out his own tongue and is stricken dead by divine means because "il ot vne pieche fait si forte fin si chai mort a la terre" (Sommer I: 221), "he dared to make a sin to so strong an end that he fell dead on the ground".

Lucan commits his sin with rhetoric; he applies the logic of earthly grammar to the description of the Virgin Mary's nature, which renders his meaning false. Josephus defeats him by applying the right, heavenly, grammar to talk to, rather than merely about, the Virgin Mary to demonstrate his rightness to the audience both embedded within the narrative and the actual reader of *The History of the Holy Grail*. Unlike the earlier doublet of this explanation of the Virgin Mary's perpetual virginity, the introduction of the metaphor is also a metaphor for the correct rules to interpret the following metaphor.

This forms a parallel between Josephus' defense of the virtue of the Virgin Mary using his holy powers of faith and Merlin's use of the opposite, his demonic powers of rhetoric, in defense of the sexual virtue of his mother. It also forms an inverted parallel to the representative of rhetoric in the same story, Lucan, who uses rhetoric to attack the virtue of the Virgin Mary. Merlin and Lucan are both masculine interpreters of a

feminine text, which is the character of Merlin's mother or the Virgin

Mary. Merlin even makes the same accusation to his mother's judge that

Lucan makes to the Virgin Mary (Sommer II: 15-17), namely that they

had illicit sex to produce their sons. The difference is that Lucan is

incorrect in his assertion and Merlin is correct, and that makes the

difference in the outcome for each of them.

The metaphor of the lily and rosebush itself is straightforward. It

describes Ambrosius' stance on the Virgin Mary and it is an incident

from Ganor's youth that Josephus knows of through supernatural insight

despite its secrecy. Ganor the young cowherd sees a large rosebush grow

out of a lily. The lily bleeds red on the rosebush and all the roses wither

and fall; only one rose is unaffected and grows for nine days. On the

ninth day, Ganor is hurt by a boar and sees a figure come out of the rose

and get immediately attacked by a serpent, which he kills. The figure

walks away with the lily. Ganor kisses the rose from which he sprang and

is healed, then when Ganor held the rose "& tu la uoloies ouurir"

(Sommer I: 222), "and you [Ganor] wanted to open it"; a fiery man from

the sky takes the rose and tells Ganor "que la senefiance de la uir[fol. 59, c col. a]ge ne deuoies tu pas[24] o toi porter puis que tu nestoies de sa

creance" (Sommer I: 222), "because of the significance of the virgin you

must not dare[25] to carry [it] with you anymore because you are not of her

belief". The prelude is doubtless also meant to tell the reader that Ganor's

desire to open the rose is not meant to be read as sexual innuendo, but as

Ganor heedlessly seeking the source of the figure.

Josephus explains the metaphor: the lily is Eve, the rosebush the

world, the roses the prophets before Jesus who remained in Hell until

Mary's birth because of Eve's sin, the special rose is Mary who remained

a virgin after giving birth to Jesus, the figure is Jesus, the serpent is the

Devil or Death (Sommer I: 222-223). Their actions describe humanity's

history in relation to God. The metaphor is also strongly gendered as

feminine: it begins with Eve and ends with Mary, it prefers to refer to

Jesus with the grammatically feminine word, la figure, and represents the

male prophets of the Old Testament with feminine roses. This forms a

contrast between the masculine, human, interpretors of the metaphor and

feminine, nonhuman metaphorical figures. It also contrasts with the

---

[24] Variant reading noted in Sommer: auoir auueques toi.
[25] Variant translation: have [it] with you.

metaphor of Mary's virginity shown to king Evalach: it is complex and broad in its scope, speaking of much that is beside the main point, and unnaturally twists the gender of the metaphorical signs from matching their referents; from these differences, the metaphor given king Evalach can be called a metaphor of faith, and the metaphor given duke Ganor a metaphor of rhetoric.

The *Arthurian Vulgate* presents its text as rhetoric in stories that purport to record public speeches at court: Merlin's defense of his mother and the False Guinevere's claim of the throne engage with text as rhetoric in contrast to the descriptions of wandering knights' reports of their adventures at court which are presented as denotative reports of fact. Outside of the *Arthurian Vulgate* the report of a knight returned from adventure is scrutinized, particularly in Chrétien de Troyes' *Yvain, or the Knight of the Lion*. Yvain feels obliged to find a way to prove his victory before he describes it publicly so that he will not be vulnerable to his peers doubting the truth of his prowess. This skepticism is externalized through Kay's mocking speech, which Yvain will have to refute in order for his defeat of the knight of the spring to count towards building his reputation. The description of Yvain's mental state in indirect discourse

says as much:

> Qu'il crient se paine avoir perdue
>
> Se mort ou vif ne le detient,
>
> Que des rampornes li souvient
>
> Que mesire Keus li ot dites.
>
> N'iert pas de la pramesse quites
>
> C'a son cousin avoit promises,
>
> Ne creüs n'iert en nule guise
>
> Se enseignes vraies n'en porte. (68d.883)
>
> He feared that his effort had been lost
>
> His death or life did not detain him,
>
> Since he remembered the mockery
>
> That sir Kay had told him.
>
> He will not repay the promise
>
> He had made to his cousin,
>
> He will not be believed in any way
>
> If he does not bring true proof.

The *Arthurian Vulgate* does not explore this need for a knight to present

evidence of his tales in stories original to it, usually reduplications of older stories. At several points, it even describes its own composition as a recording of a knight's report at court by having a clerk present at court write down the knight's story. In stories that are transmitted from tradition, the knight speaks[26] and/or presents witnesses at court who are present at the telling with him or sends prisoners or other messengers to court ahead of himself to tell the court what happened. Within the narrative, the *Book of Merlin*'s existence is explained as the recording of Ambrosius Blaise, who writes down what he witnesses and what Merlin transmits to him (Sommer II: 19). In this way, the *Arthurian Vulgate* presents itself as a collection of stories that may or may not describe real events in the world; the contentious rhetoric that draws attention to the gaps between reality and its telling, like the False Guinevere episode and the trial of Merlin's mother, is focused on the object of female virtue.

---

[26] An example: Guinevere tells the repeat of the *Chevalier de la Charette*'s interpolation to Arthur (Sommer IV: 320).

Conclusions

In conclusion, the *Odyssey* and the *Arthurian Vulgate* are very different regarding how they handle gender. The *Odyssey* is concerned with finding parallels and equal worth between men and women in gendered roles without attaching it to the value of either gender to the gods. The *Arthurian Vulgate* is concerned with promoting an ideal of gendered roles being a part of one's religious obligations and encouraging people to conform to them. Another major difference is that the *Odyssey* is more concerned with presenting distinct individual characters than the *Arthurian Vulgate*, which emphasizes individual characters' identity with generic character types. Both of them, as befits compositions formed from traditional material, contain contradictory gender constructions. They also both apply different standards to the gendered behaviour of their characters depending on their status as a human being, a monster, a god, a demon, or a rhetorical figure.

The *Odyssey* parallels masculine and feminine uses of the power of speech. Both male and female characters derive power from it to a degree determined by their divinity or humanity. Human speech is a characteristic of women in civilized society and a power of the nymphs

Circe and Calypso. The epithets χρυσόθρονος and ἐύθρονος mark

contexts which would concern a high-status woman seated publicly in a

hall, when applied to Eos in a day-opening line, the epithet marks the

day's action. The lion and outgoing sociability are gendered masculine,

and inwardly-focused sociability is gendered feminine. The masculine

and the feminine are paralleled both through direct comparisons between

Odysseus and Penelope and through the competitions with characters of

the opposite gender that Odysseus and Penelope each eventually win:

Odysseus against Circe and Calypso and Penelope against the suitors.

Feminine characteristics are not applied to contexts absent a female

character, be she a human, a monster, a goddess, or a stock figure.

The *Arthurian Vulgate*, despite its ideological priorities towards

the ideal man and husband serving God and his secular responsibilities

and the ideal woman and wife serving her husband and God, has both

preserved and warped within itself contradictory ideals from its sources.

The more strongly an episode original to the 13th century *Arthurian prose

cycle* is written to convince the reader to espouse an ideal, the more

strongly it is gendered. It also forms correspondences between the

masculine/feminine gender binary and other contrasting binaries to form relationships within and between episodes: linking the masculine gender to the self, human beings, interpretation, and leadership, and the feminine gender to the other, text, subordination, and supernatural beings. It uses the grammatical gender of words as well as their referents to form the links to gender. Traditional stories that place female characters in a position of power over male characters are transmitted along with stories that follow the set of gender correspondences contemporary to the text. Overall, the *Arthurian prose cycle* is much more willing than the *Odyssey* to disconnect femininity in the abstract from an actual female character.

Sources Consulted

Primary Sources

Annales Cambriae. Last modified: 2013
https://la.wikisource.org/wiki/Annales_Cambriae

Chrétien de Troyes.*Yvain ou le Chevalier au Lion*
https://fr.wikisource.org/wiki/Yvain_ou_le_Chevalier_au_Lion

Chrétien de Troyes. *Le Chevalier de la Charette* ed. Godefroi de Leigni. Belinfante (1850)

Geoffery of Monmouth. *Vita Merlini*: http://www.sacred-texts.com/neu/eng/vm/vmlat.htm

Gildas. *"The Works of Gildas, Surnamed 'Sapiens,' or the Wise", in Six Old English Chronicles of Which Two Are Now First Translated from the Monkish Latin Originals: Ethelwerd's Chronicle, Asser's Life of Alfred, Geoffrey of Monmouth's British History, Gildas, Nennius, and Richard of Cirencester*. Ed. John Allen Giles. London: Henry G. Bohn, 1848.

Hammer, Jacob/ Geoffrey of Monmouth, *Historia regum Britanniae*, a variant version.
Edited by JACOB HAMMER. Medieval Academy Books, No. 57 (1951).

Homer. *Homeri Opera in five volumes*. Oxford, Oxford University Press. 1920.

Homer. *The Odyssey with an English Translation by A.T. Murray, PH.D. in two volumes*. Cambridge, MA., Harvard University Press; London, William Heinemann, Ltd. 1919.

Marie de France. *Lais de Marie de France*. ed. Karl Warnke, Max Niemeyer (Blibliotheca Normannica), 1900.

Polyglot Bible. http://www.sacred-texts.com/bib/poly/index.htm

Saxo Grammaticus. *Gesta Danorum*. Ed. Alfred Holder. Strassburg: Verlag Von Karl J. Trubner. 1886.

Sommer, H. Oskar. *The vulgate version of the Arthurian romances.*
Washington : Carnegie Institution of Washington 1909.

The Mabinogion. translated by Lady Charlotte Guest. 1877. Accessed at:
https://en.wikisource.org/wiki/The_Mabinogion

Welsh Triads, translated by W. F. Skene from Peniarth MS 54 (1868):
https://en.wikisource.org/wiki/Welsh_Triads/Peniarth_MS_54

Welsh Triads, translated by John Rhys and J. Gwenogvryn Evans from
the Red Book of Hergest (1887):
https://en.wikisource.org/wiki/Welsh_Triads/Red_Book_of_Hergest

Secondary Sources

A Dictionary of the Welsh Language. University of Wales 2016.
http://geiriadur.ac.uk/gpc/gpc.html

Autenrieth, Georg. *A Homeric Dictionary for Schools and Colleges*. New
York. Harper and Brothers. 1891.

Beekes, R. S. P. *Etymological Dictionary of Greek*. Brill, 2009.

Campbell, Joseph. *The Hero with a Thousand Faces.* Princeton:
Princeton University Press, 1968

De Looze, Laurence. "The Problem of Look-alike Characters in the
Vulgate Cycle of the Arthurian Romances and Juan Manuel's *El Conde
Lucanor*" in *Comparative Literature* 2014 Volume 66, Number 2: 173-
185.

Dio Chrysostom *Discourses* in Loeb Classical Library, 5 volumes, Greek
texts and facing English translation: Harvard University Press,
1932 thru 1951. Translation by J. W. Cohoon thru Or. 31; the remainder
by H. Lamar Crosby.

Duggan, Joseph J. *The Romances of Chrétien de Troyes*, Yale University
Press, 2001.

DMF: *Dictionnaire du Moyen Français*, version 2015 (DMF 2015).
ATILF - CNRS & Université de Lorraine. http://www.atilf.fr/dmf.

Dupraz, Joëlle et Fraisse, Christel. *Carte archéologique de la Gaule,
l'Ardèche*. Éditions de la Maison des sciences de l'homme, Paris: 1985.

Euripides. The Complete Greek Drama, edited by Whitney J. Oates and
Eugene O'Neill, Jr. in two volumes. 2. Helen, translated by E. P.
Coleridge. New York. Random House. 1938.

Fontenrose, *Orion: the Myth of the Hunter and the Huntress,* University
of California Press: 1981.

Geoffrey of Monmouth. *The Vita Merlini* translated by John Jay Parry (The University of Illinois: Urbana, 1925) University of Illinois studies in language and literature, vol. X, no. 3.

Gresseth, Gerald K. "The Odyssey and the Nalopākhyāna" in *Transactions of the American Philological Association* (1974-), Vol. 109 (1979) pp. 65-70.

Homer. The Iliad with an English Translation by A.T. Murray, Ph.D. in two volumes. Cambridge, MA., Harvard University Press; London, William Heinemann, Ltd. 1924.

Homer. The Odyssey with an English Translation by A.T. Murray, PH.D. in two volumes. Cambridge, MA., Harvard University Press; London, William Heinemann, Ltd. 1919.

Jamison, Stephanie W. "Penelope and the Pigs: Indic Perspectives on the *Odyssey*" in *Classical Antiquity* 18 (2) 1999, pg. 227-272.

Killebrew, Ann E. "Biblical Peoples and Ethnicity: An Archaeological Study of Egyptians, Canaanites, Philistines, and Early Israel, 1300–1100 B.C.E" in *Society of Biblical Lit*, 2005

Liddell and Scott. *An Intermediate Greek-English Lexicon*. Oxford. Clarendon Press. 1889.

Liddell, Henry George. Scott, Robert. *A Greek-English Lexicon. revised and augmented throughout by. Sir Henry Stuart Jones. with the assistance of. Roderick McKenzie*. Oxford. Clarendon Press. 1940.

Mahoney, Kevin. *Latdict*. 2016: http://latin-dictionary.net/

Mazon, Albin. *Voyage autour d'Annonay*. Hervé Frères: 1901.

Meyer, Leo. *Handbuch der Greischen Etymologie* 1901.

Pantelia, Maria C. "Helen and the Last Song for Hector" in *Transactions of the American Philological Association* 132.1-2 (2002) 21-27.

Pausanias. Pausanias Description of Greece with an English Translation by W.H.S. Jones, Litt.D., and H.A. Ormerod, M.A., in 4 Volumes. Cambridge, MA, Harvard University Press; London, William Heinemann Ltd. 1918.

Pindar. *Odes*. Diane Arnson Svarlien. 1990.

Richards, Melville, "Arthurian Onomastics", in: *Transactions of the Honourable Society of Cymmrodorion*, vol. 2, 1969, p. 257.

Sayers, William. "Grendel's Mother (*Beowulf*) and the Celtic Sovereignty Goddess" in *The Journal of Indo-European Studies* Vol. 35 (1&2) 2007, pp. 31-50.

Schrijver, Peter. *Studies in British Celtic Historical Phonology*. Rodopi:1995.

Singer, P. N. "Galen" in *Stanford Encyclopedia of Philosophy*.

Slater, William J. *Lexicon to Pindar*. De Gruyter, Berlin: 1969.

Strawn, Brent A. "kĕpîr' ărāyôt in Judges 14:5" in *Vetus Testamentum*, Vol. 59, Fasc. 1 (2009), pp. 150-158.

West, Emily Blanchard. "Married Hero/Single Princess: Homer's Nausicaa and the Indic Citrangada" in *The Journal of Indo-European Studies* Vol. 37 (1&2) 2009 pp. 214-224.

Younger, John G. "Review: Seals and Sealing Practices: The Ancient Near East and Bronze Age Aegaean" *American Journal of Archaeology* 100 (1996) pg. 161-165.

Author CV

Post-Secondary Education:

2010-2014: BA in Classical Studies from The University of
Western Ontario

2014-2016: MA in Comparative Literature from The University

of Western Ontario

Relevant Work Experience:

2015-2016: TA for for the course *From Homer to Picasso:*

Western Culture Across the Ages by the Department of Modern

Languages and Literatures

Publication:

"The Sibyl in Aeneid Six" International Journal of English

Literature and Culture Vol. 2. 8 (2014): 170-174.